AF258433

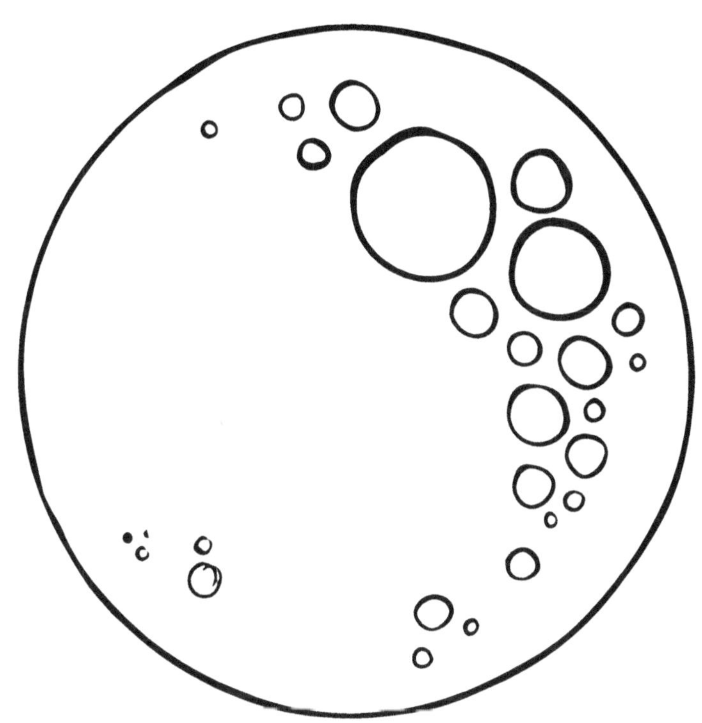

To the Moon
and Back

This project seeks to honor the human tradition of keeping time by the moon

as a basic yet fundamental tool. Any implied or perceived reference to specific

traditions, cultures or esoterica beyond this is not intended.

Feedback is welcome.

Lunar Day Planner (Undated) | Twelve Lunations

Copyright © 2021

Mara Julia Reynolds
A Flower For All Reasons Press | A Flower For All Reasons, LLC

July, 2021 | Milwaukie, Oregon

First Edition
All Rights Reserved

www.aflowerforallreasons.com
@aflowerforallreasons | #aflowerforallreasons

www.lunardayplanner.com
@lunar.dayplanner | #lunardayplanner

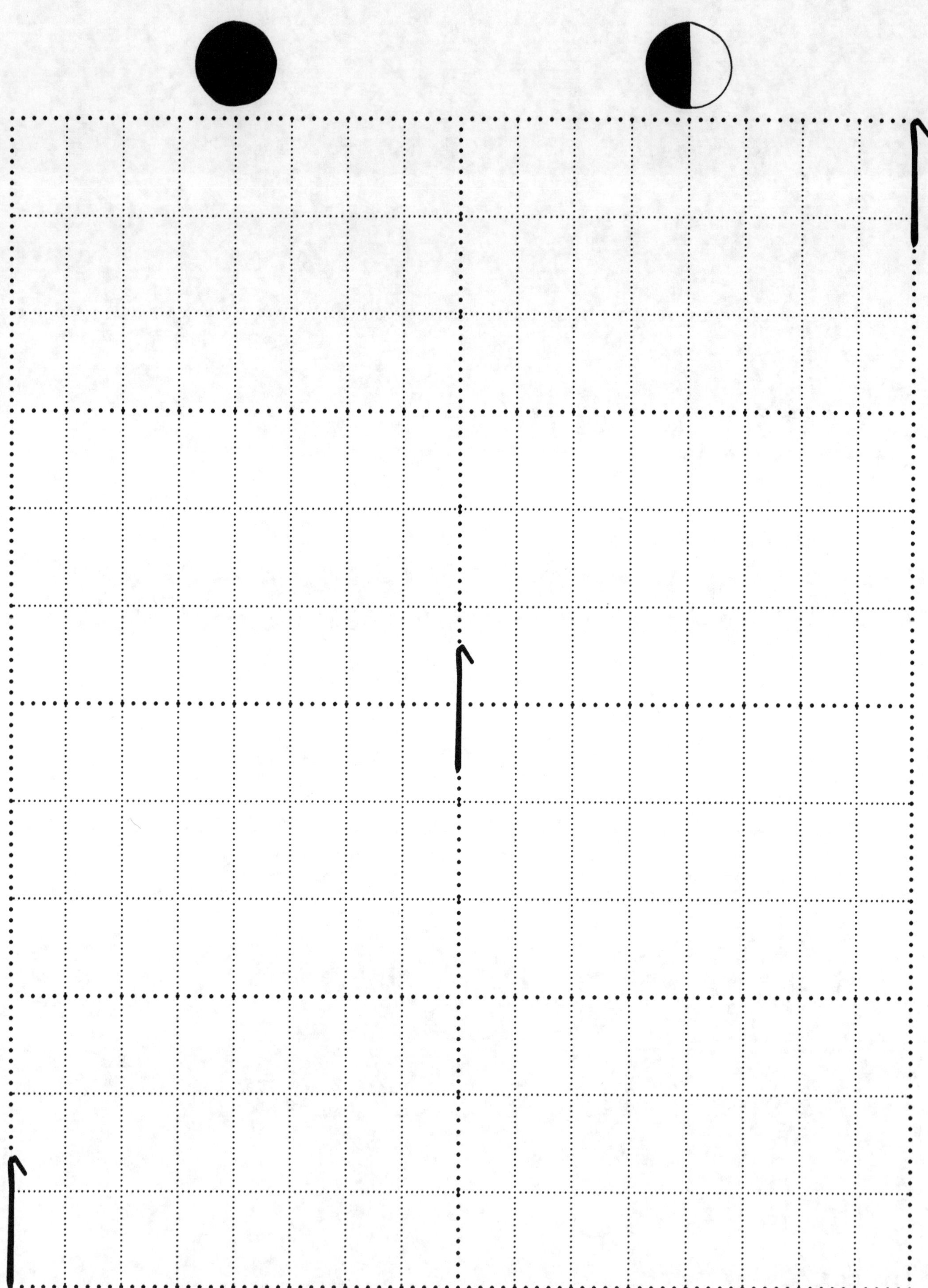

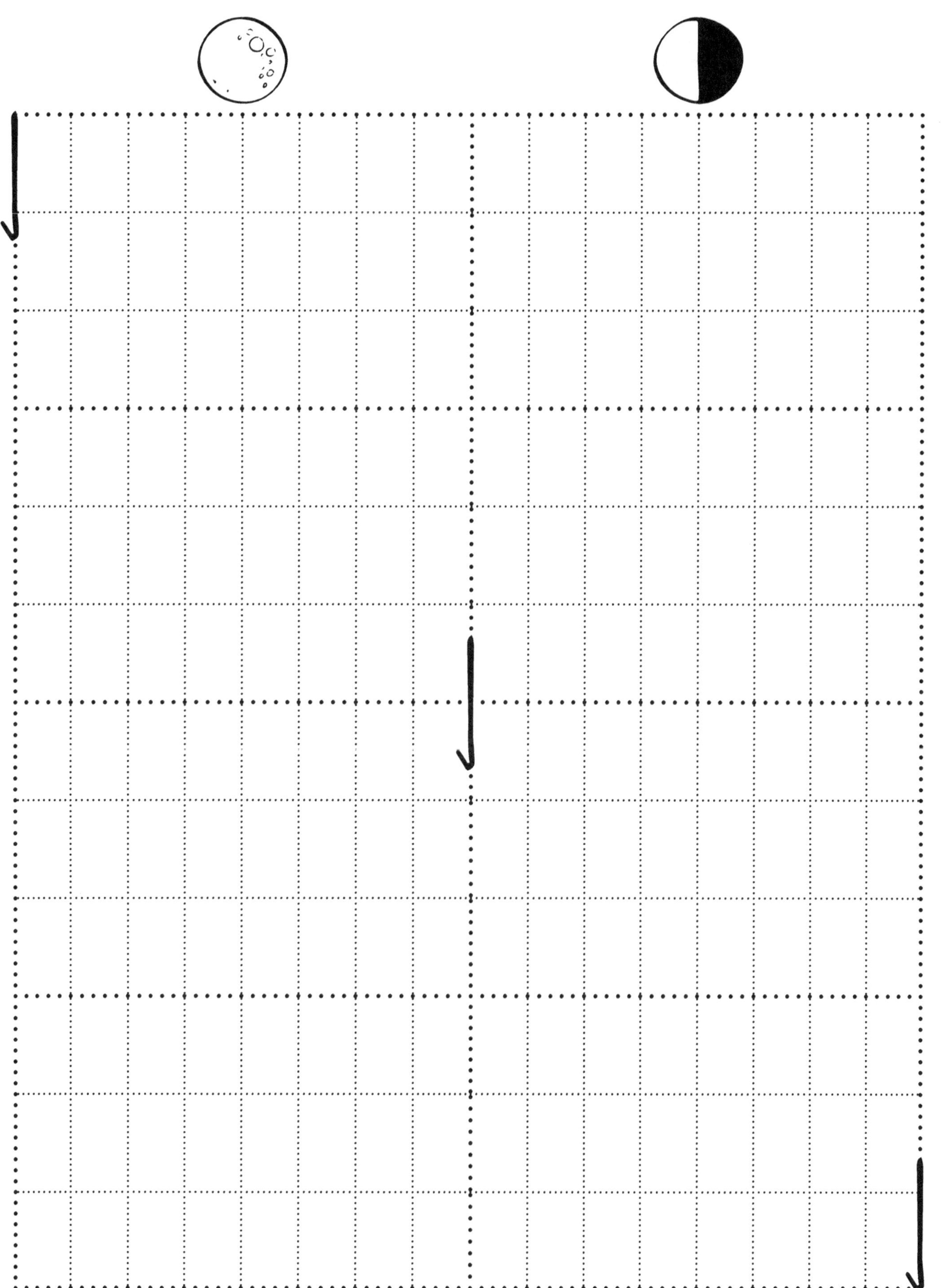

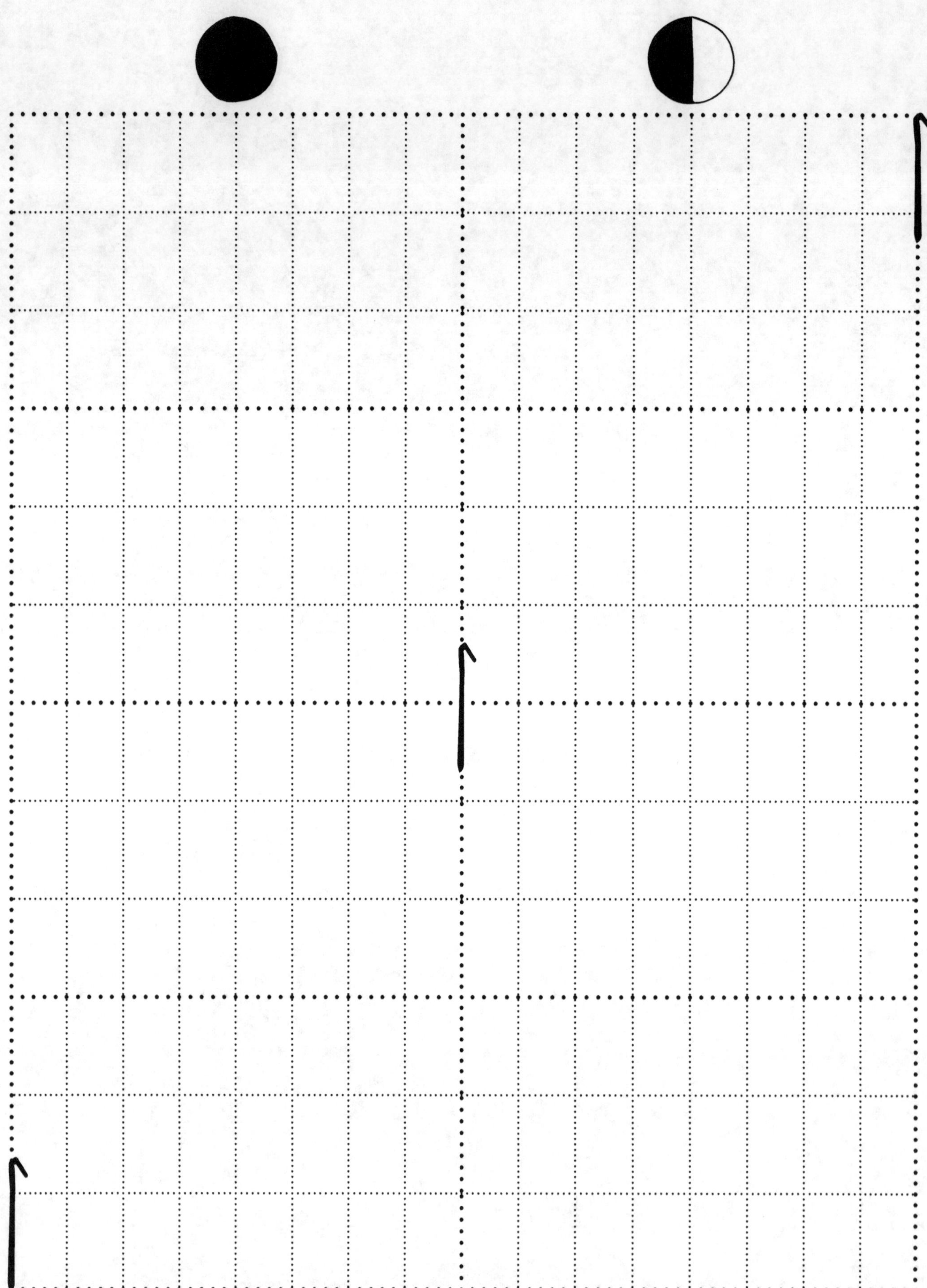

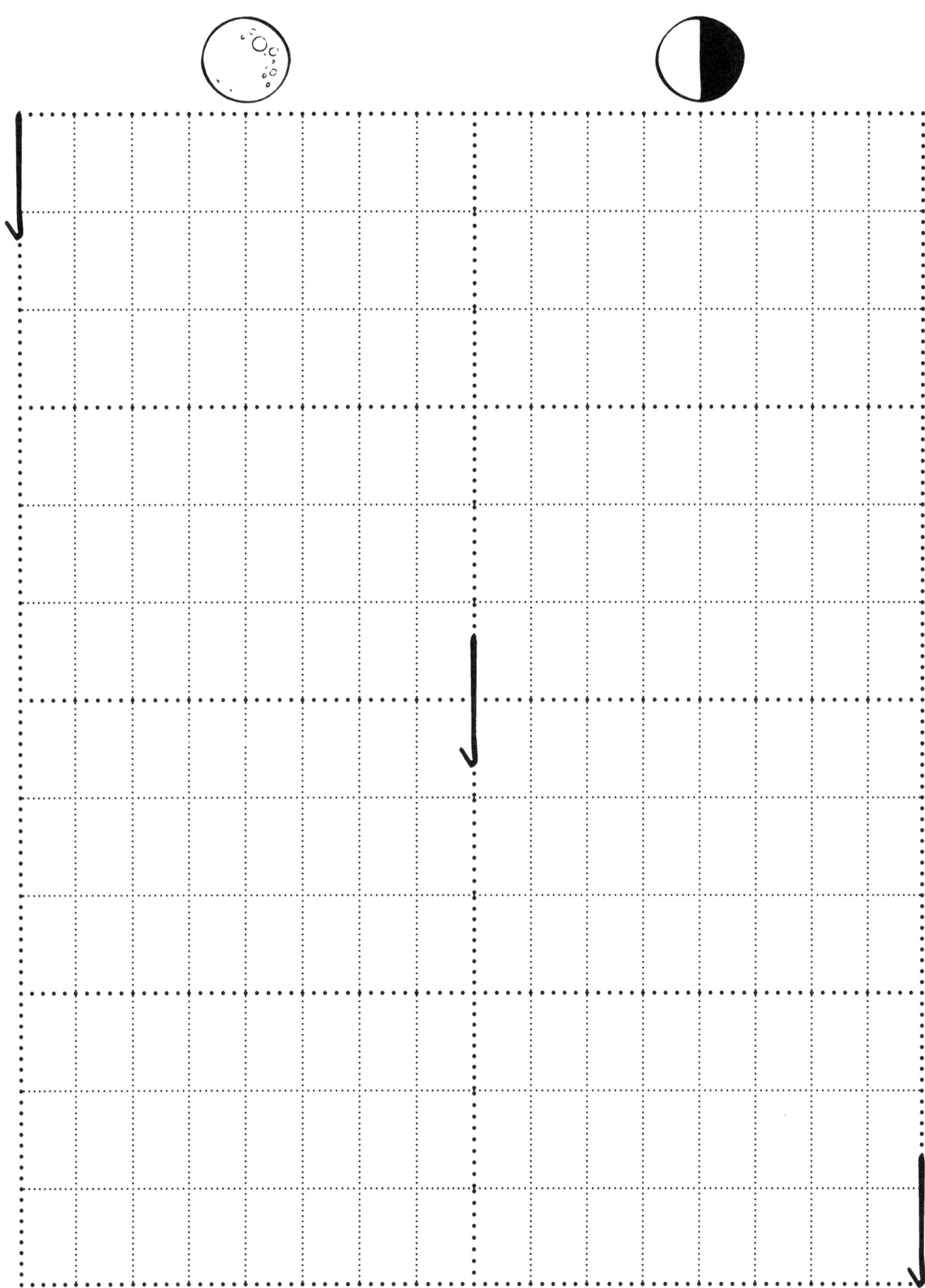

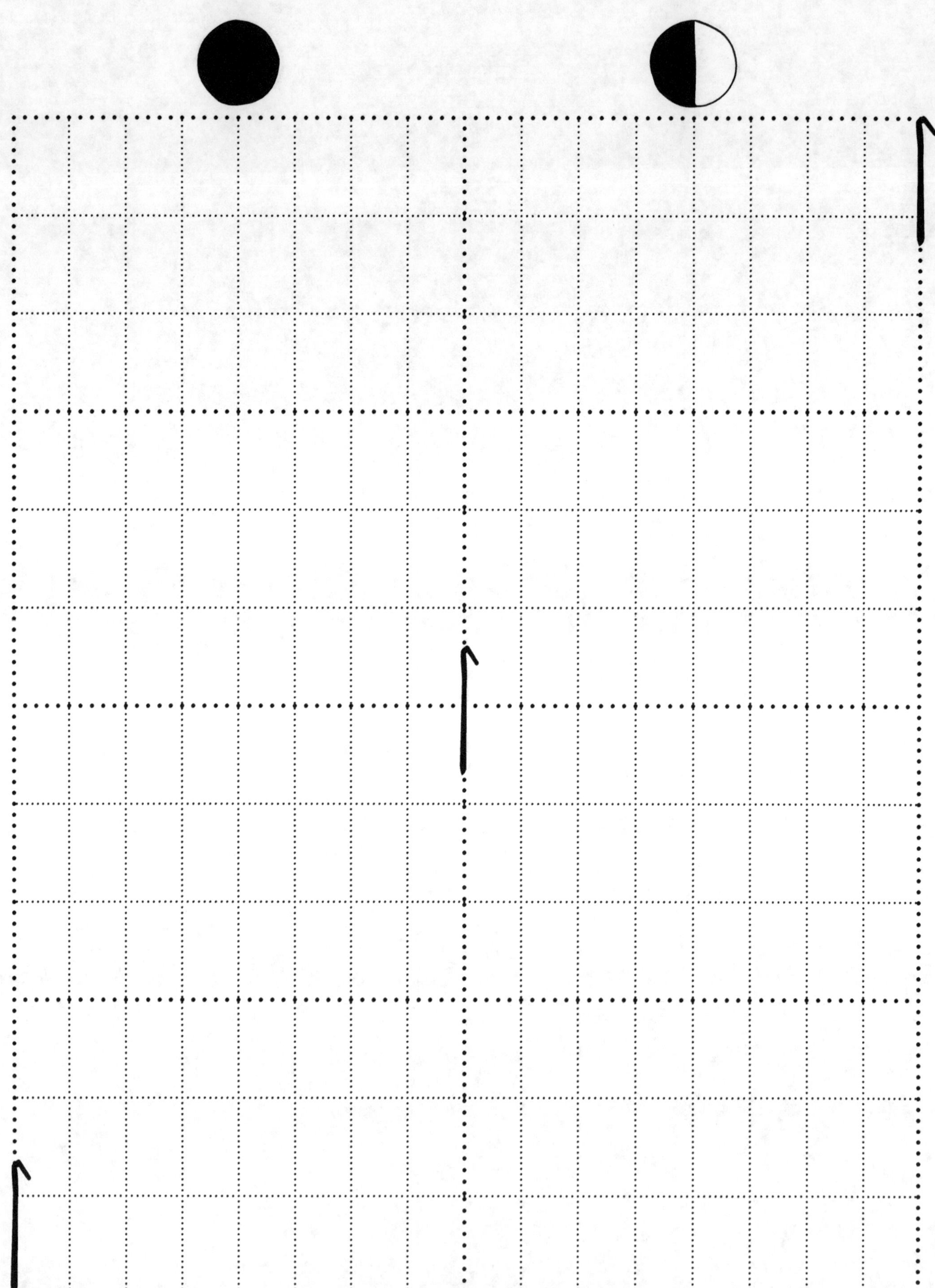

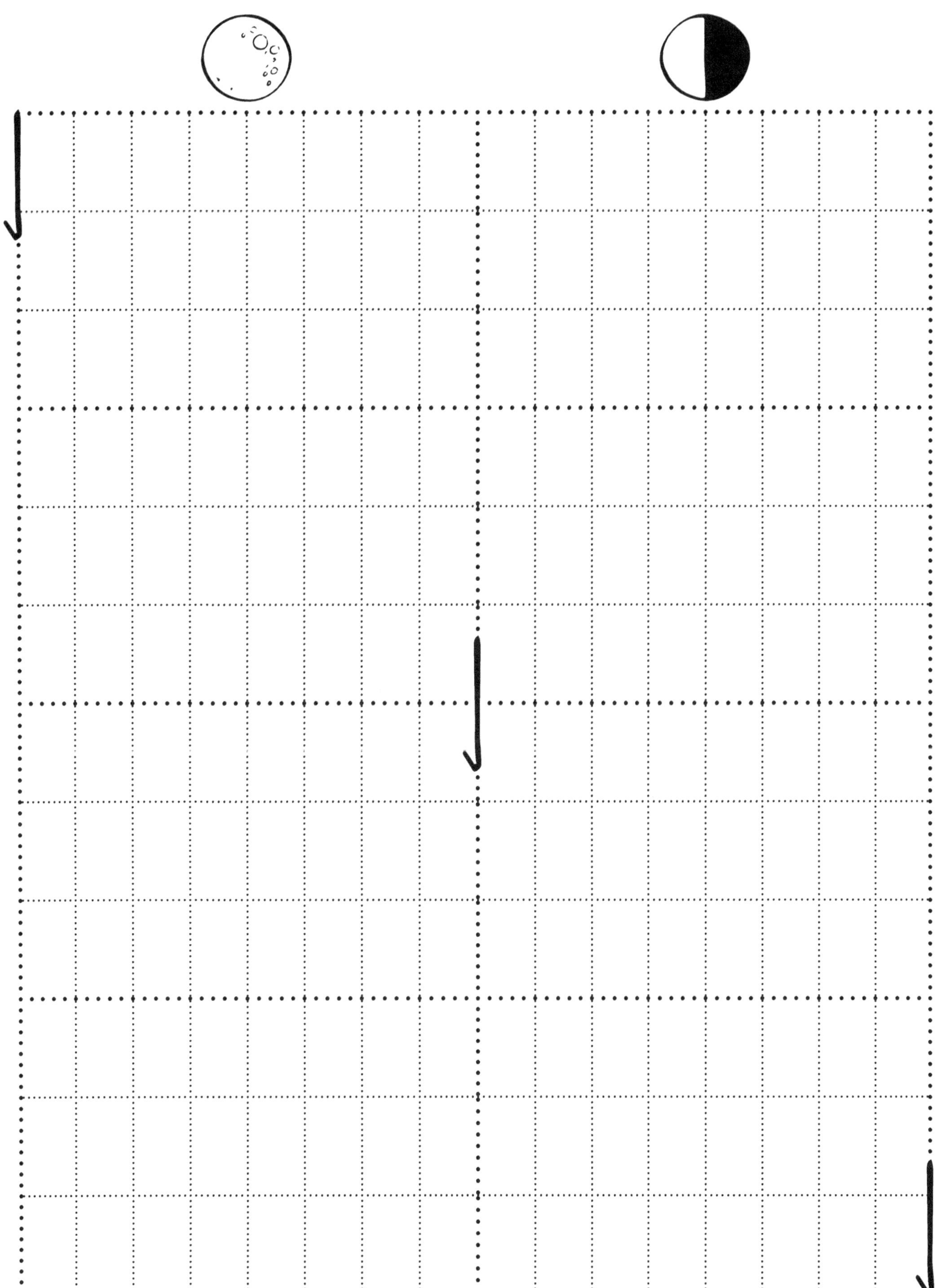

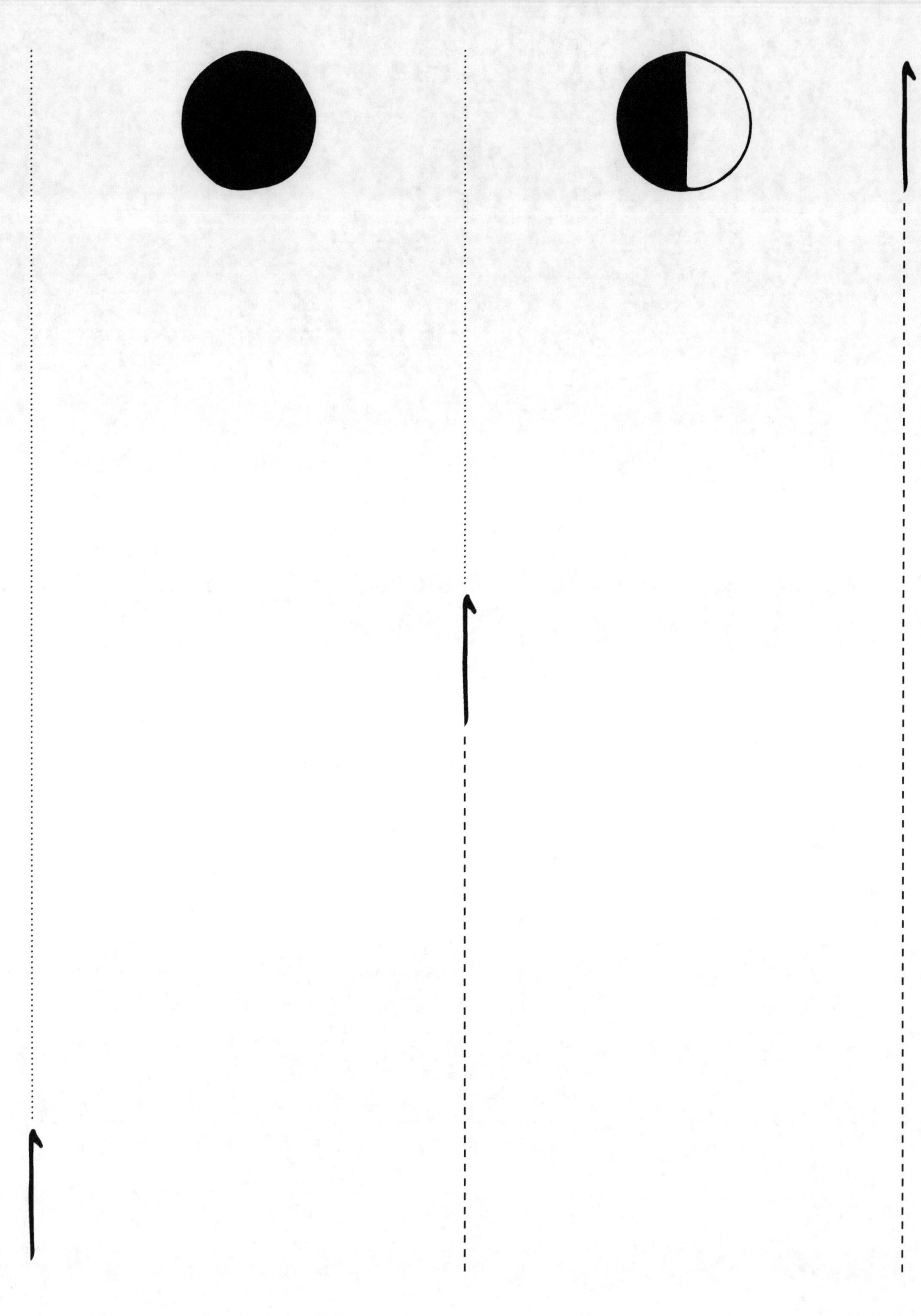

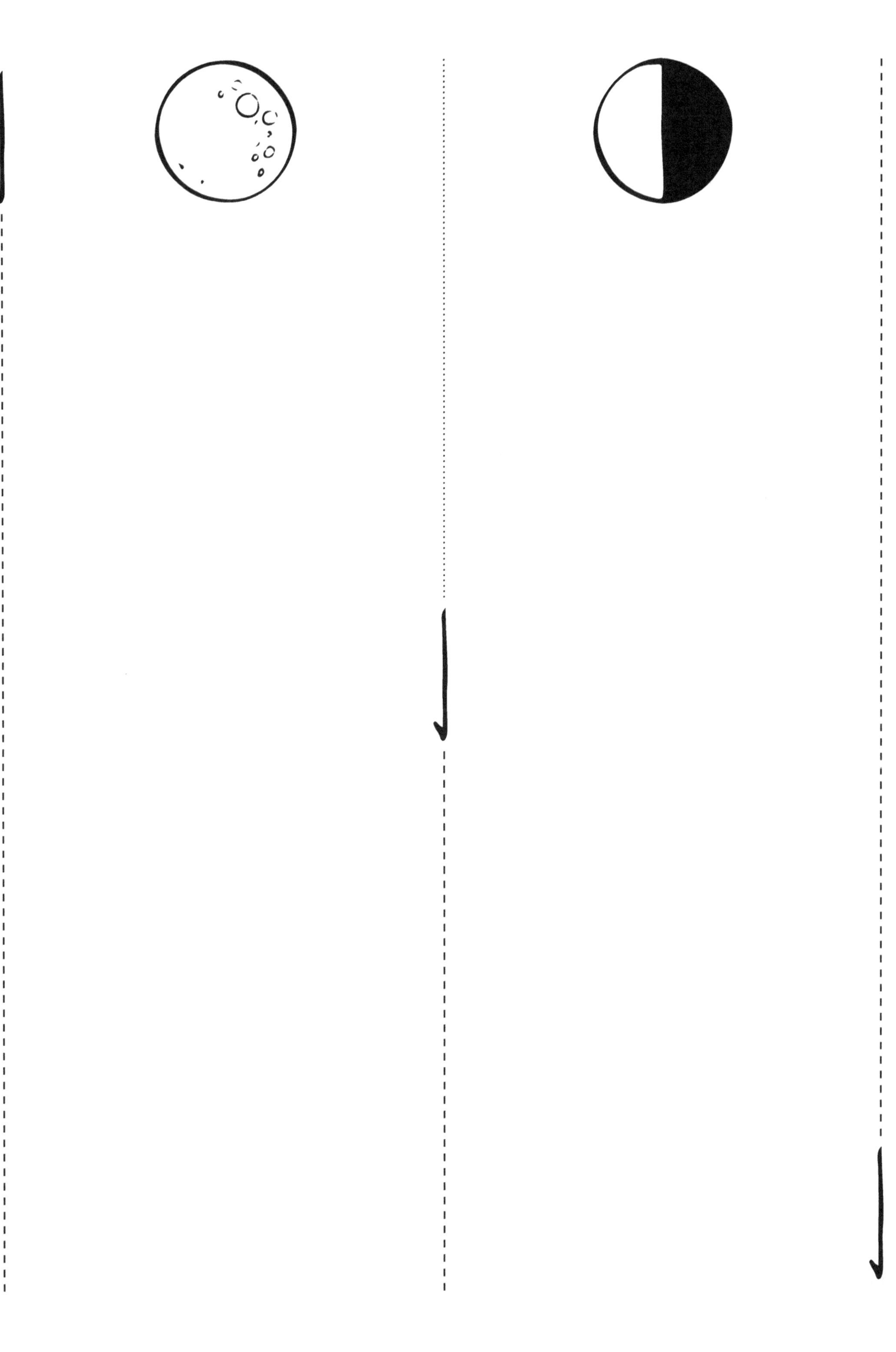

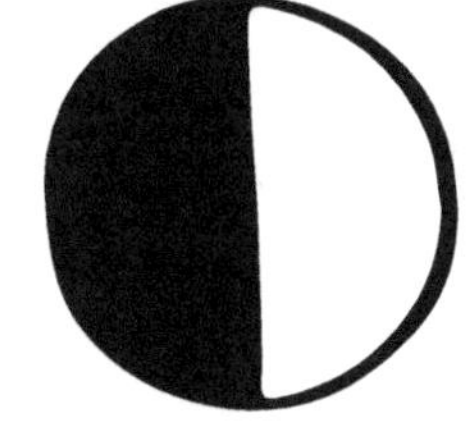

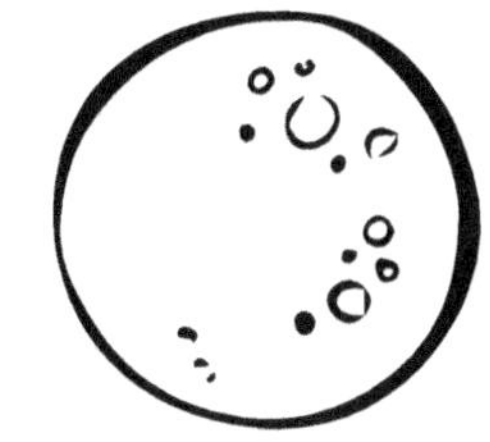

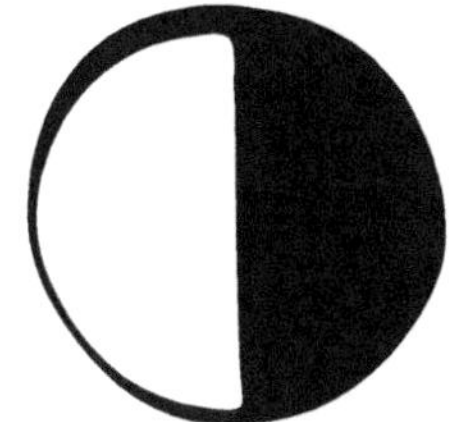

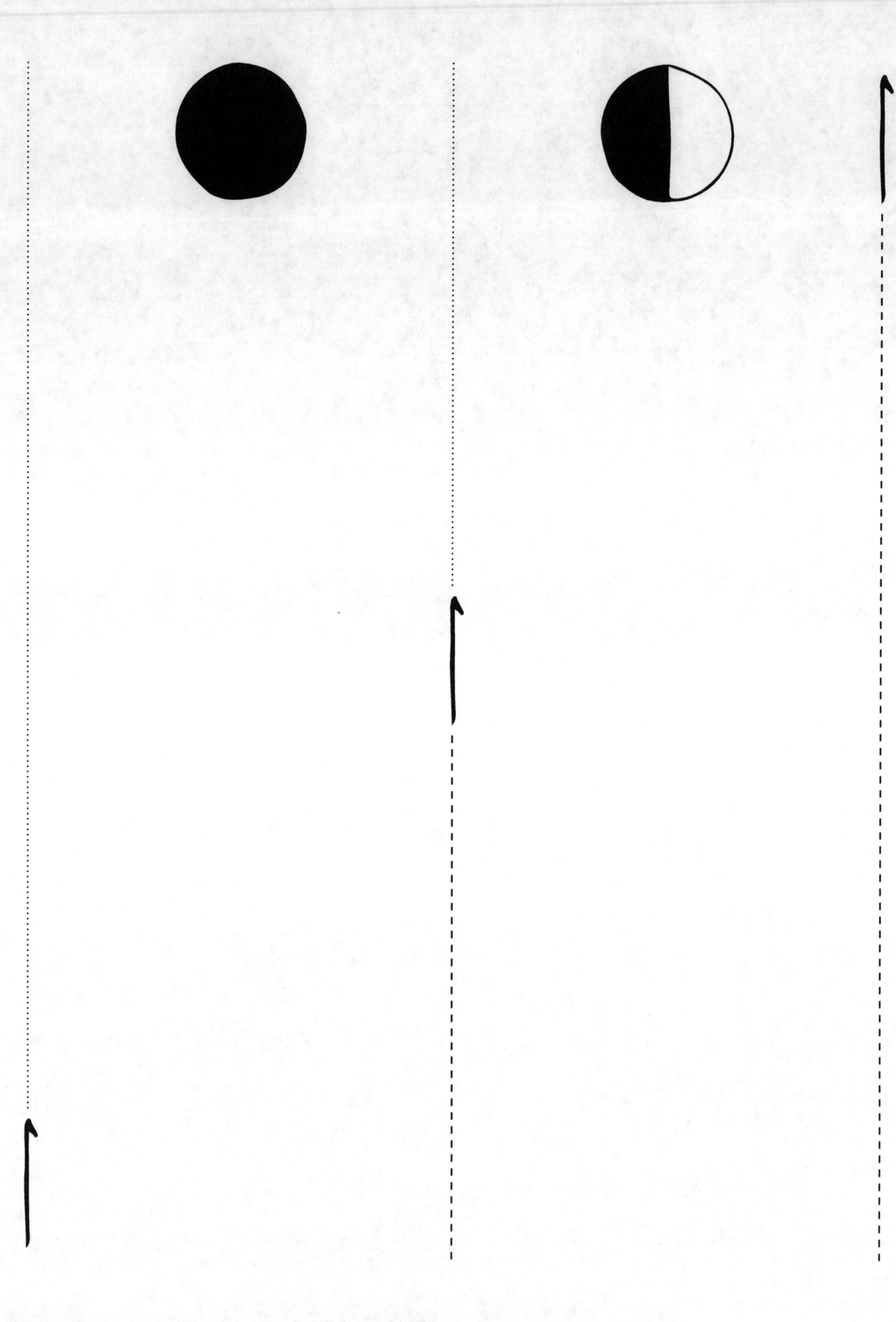

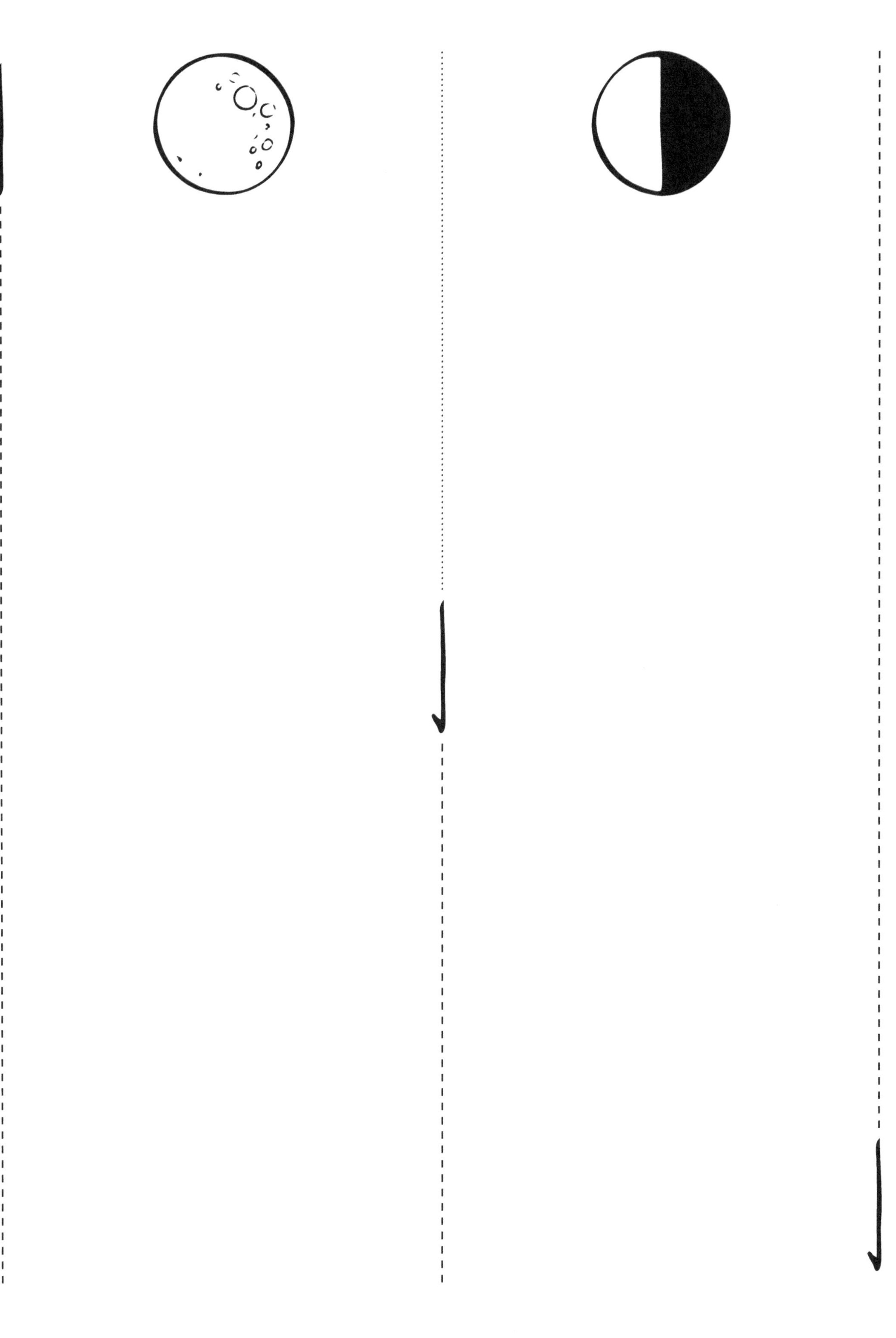

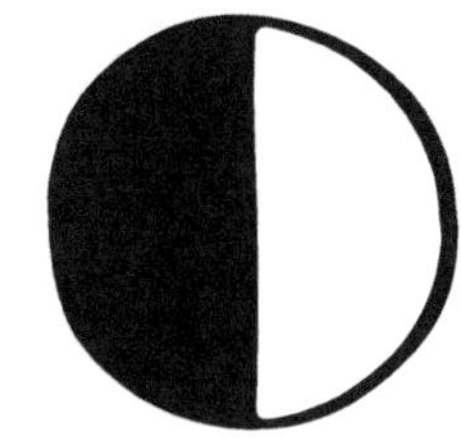

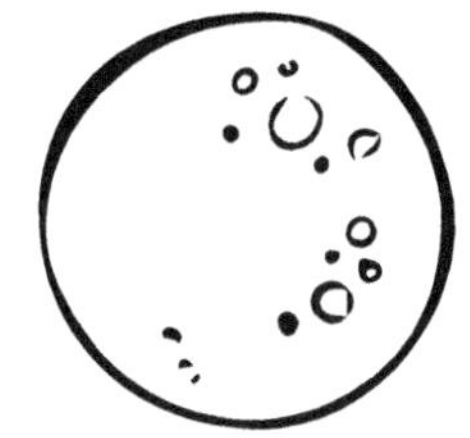

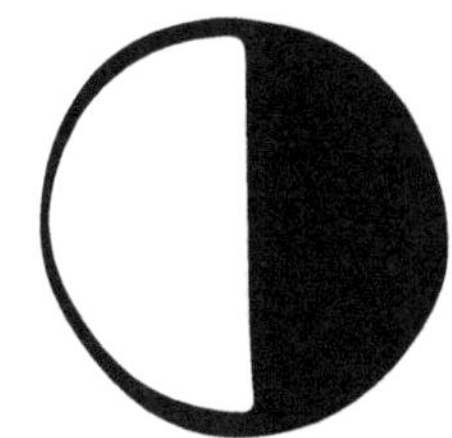

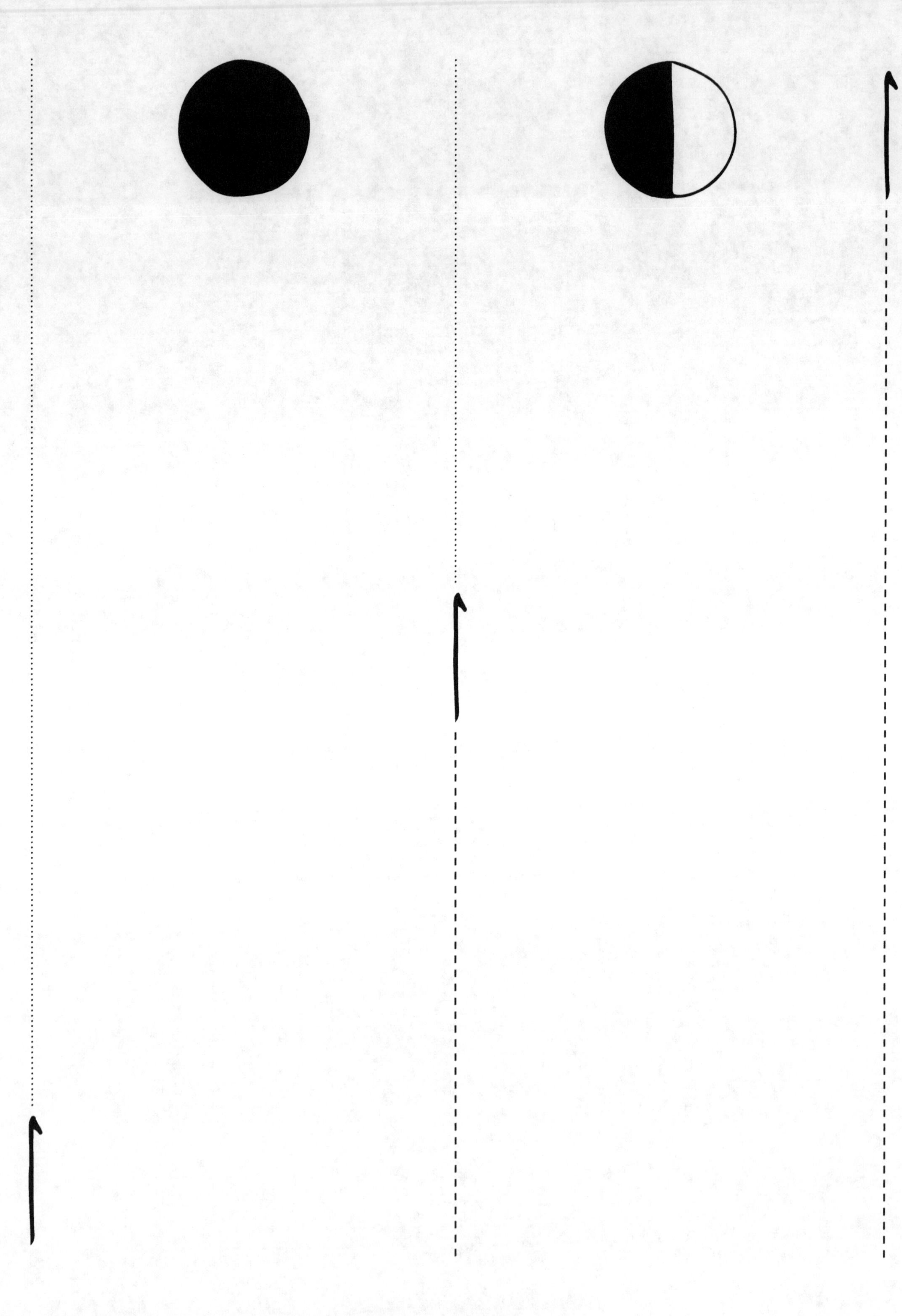

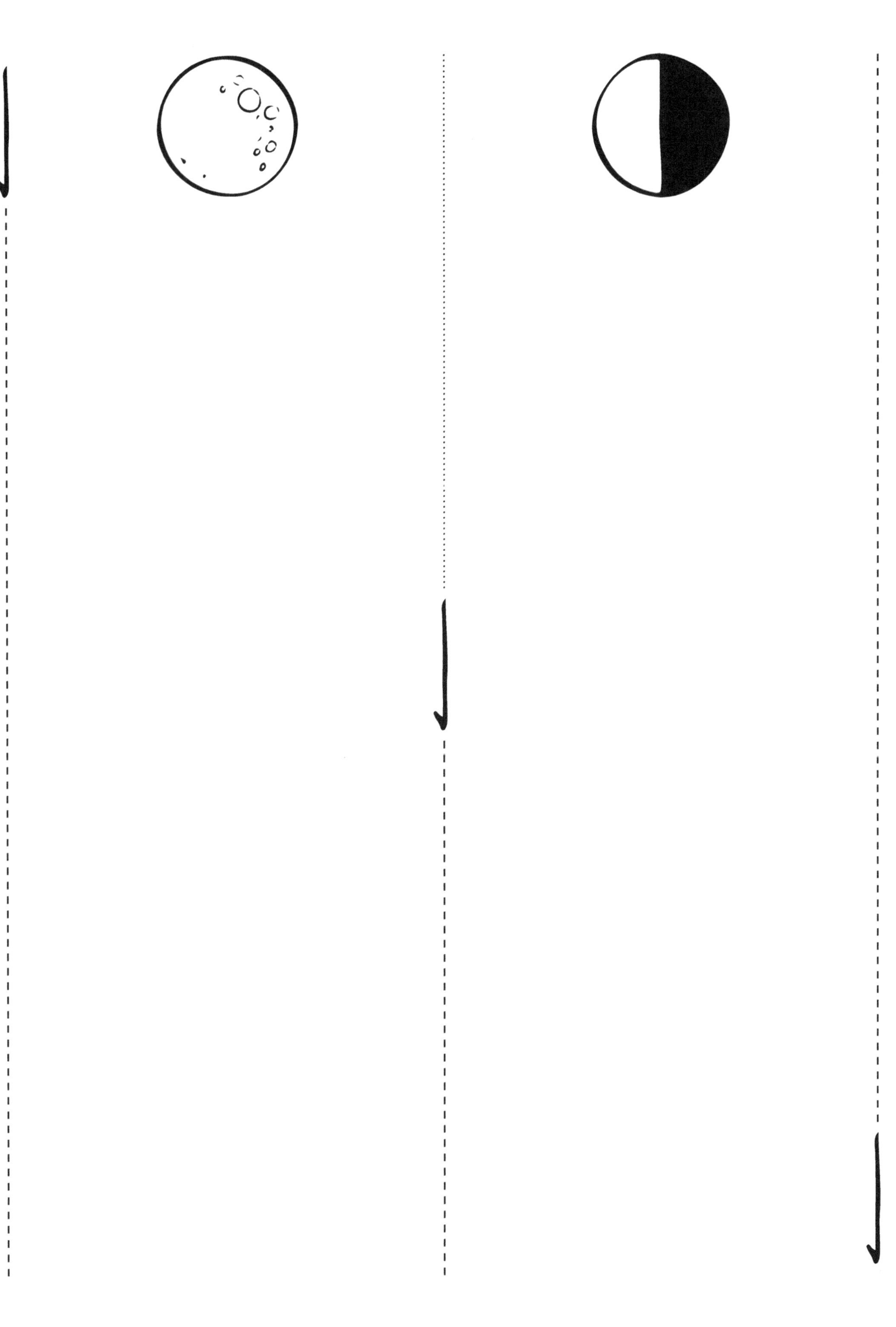

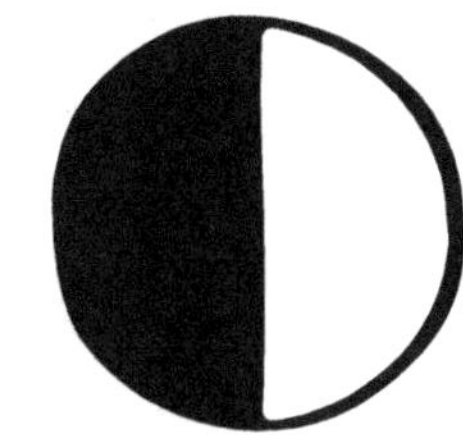

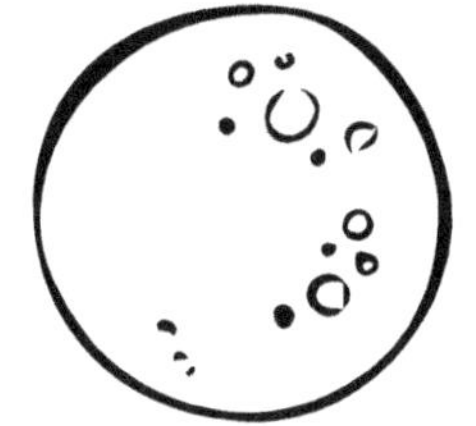

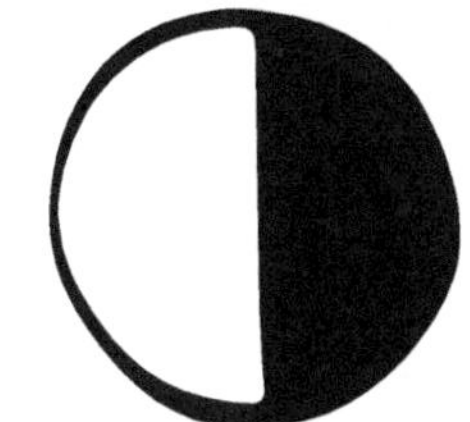

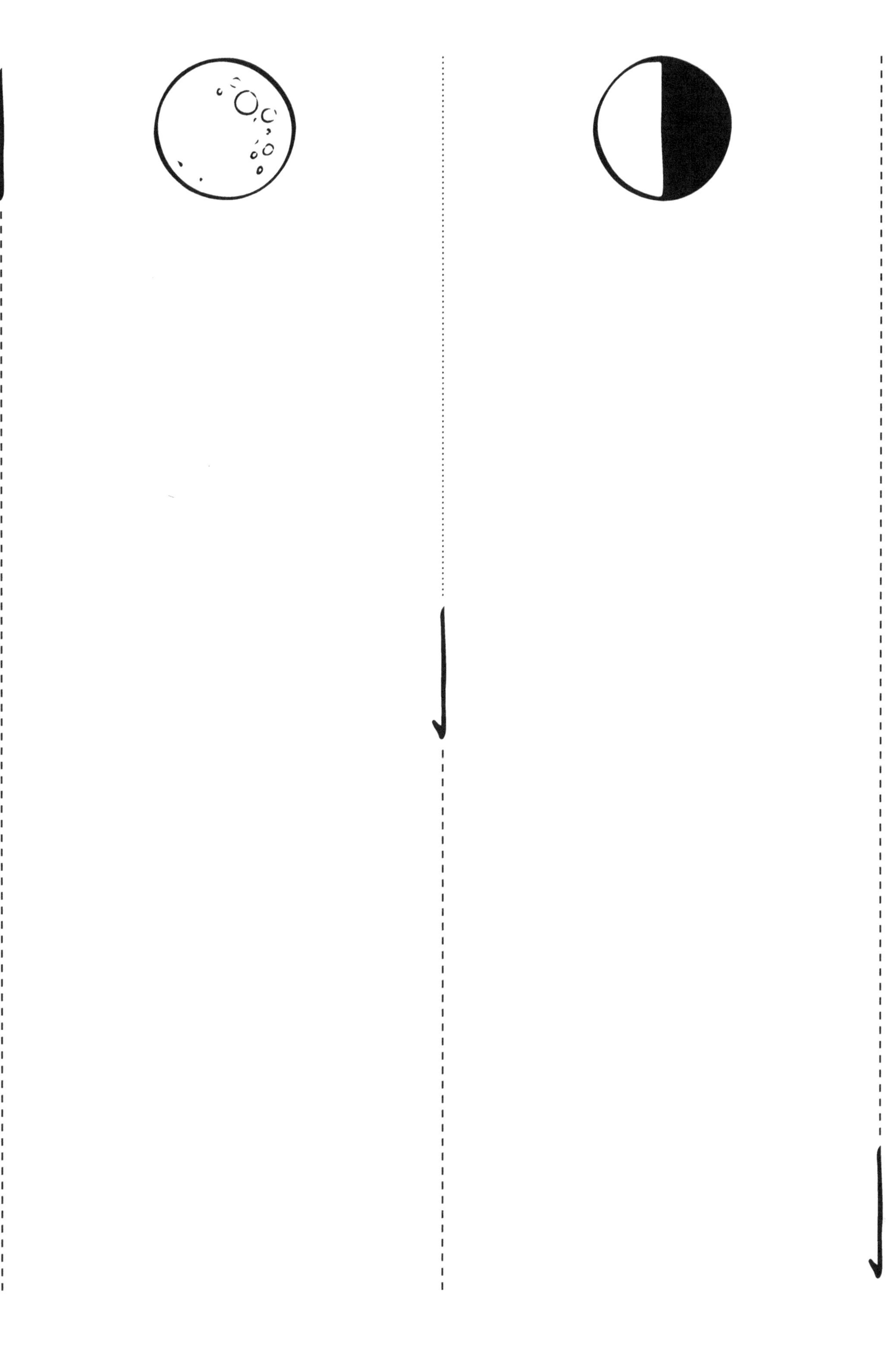

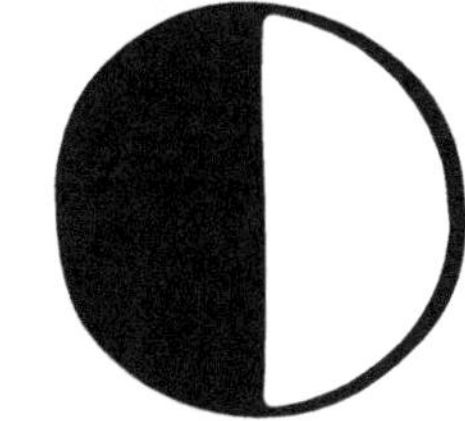

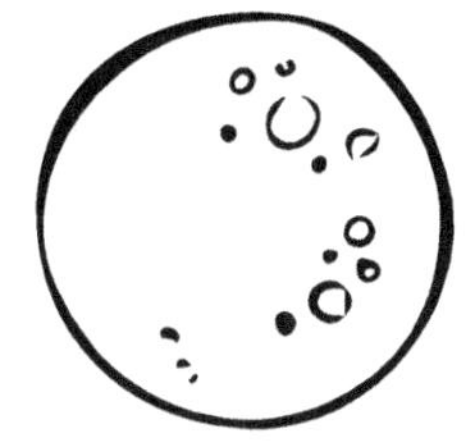

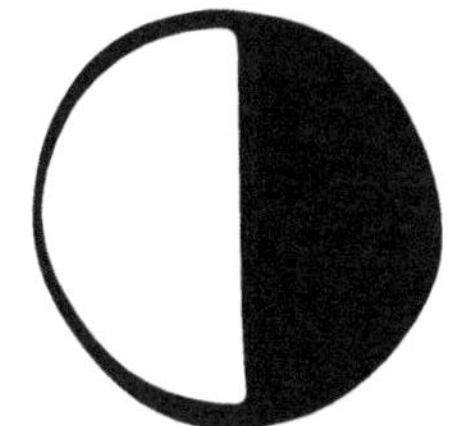

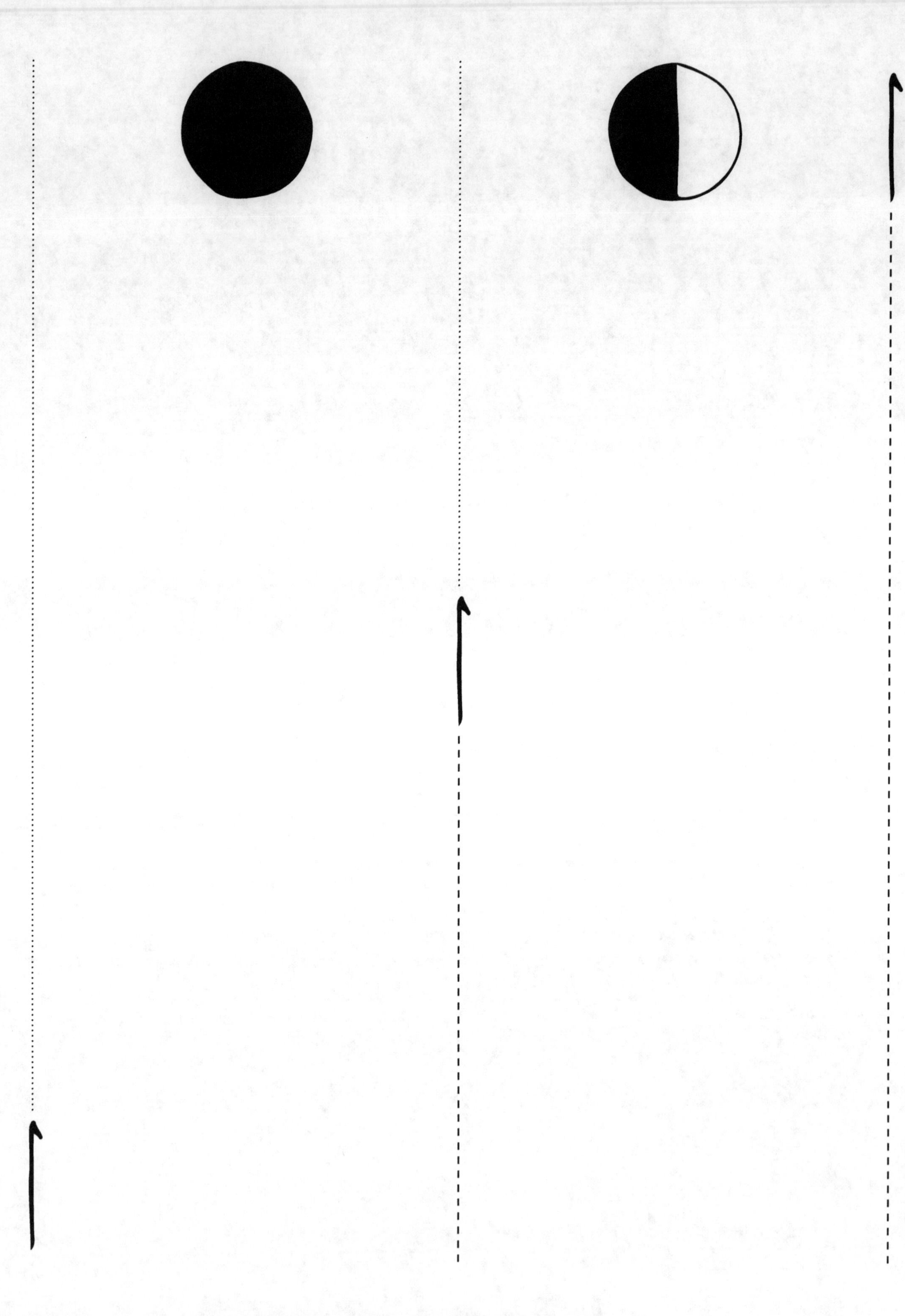

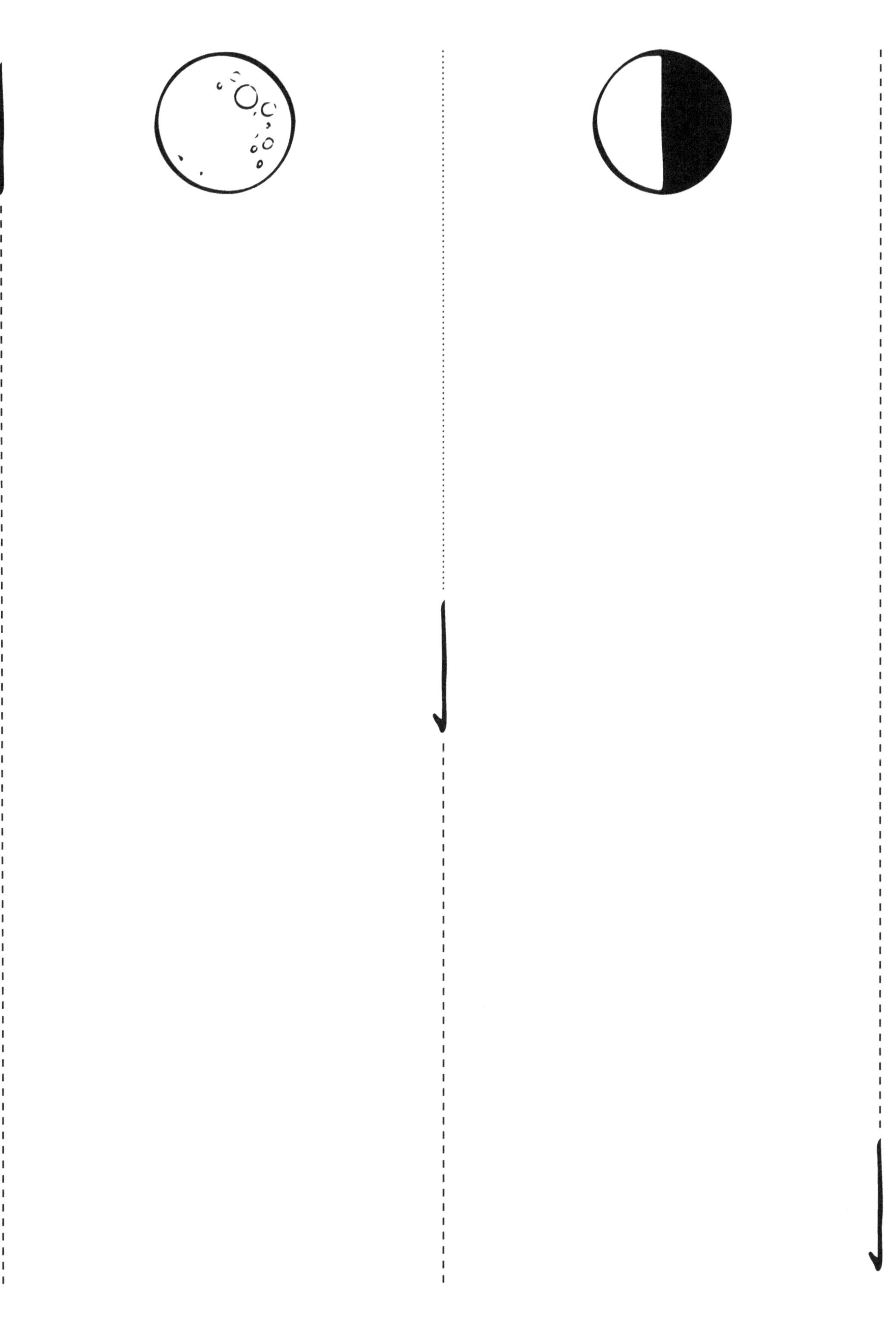

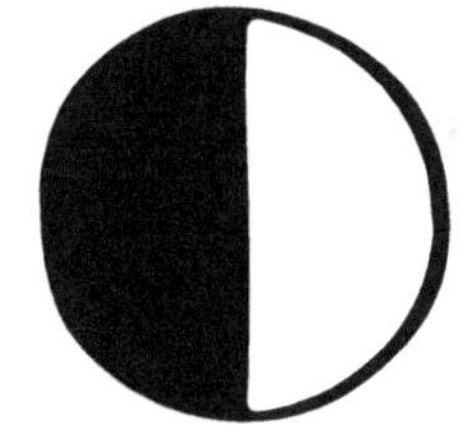

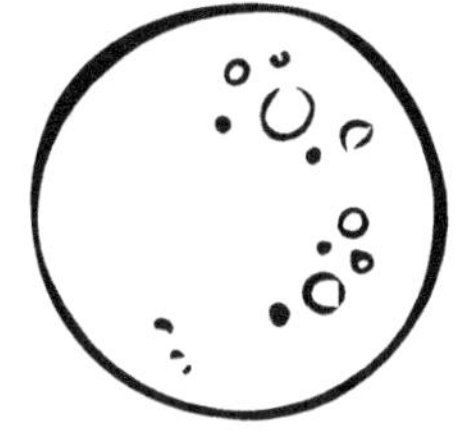

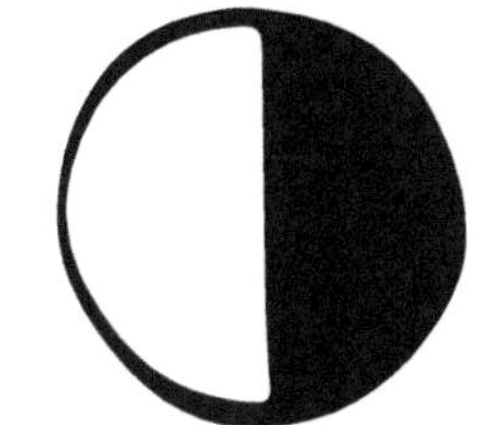

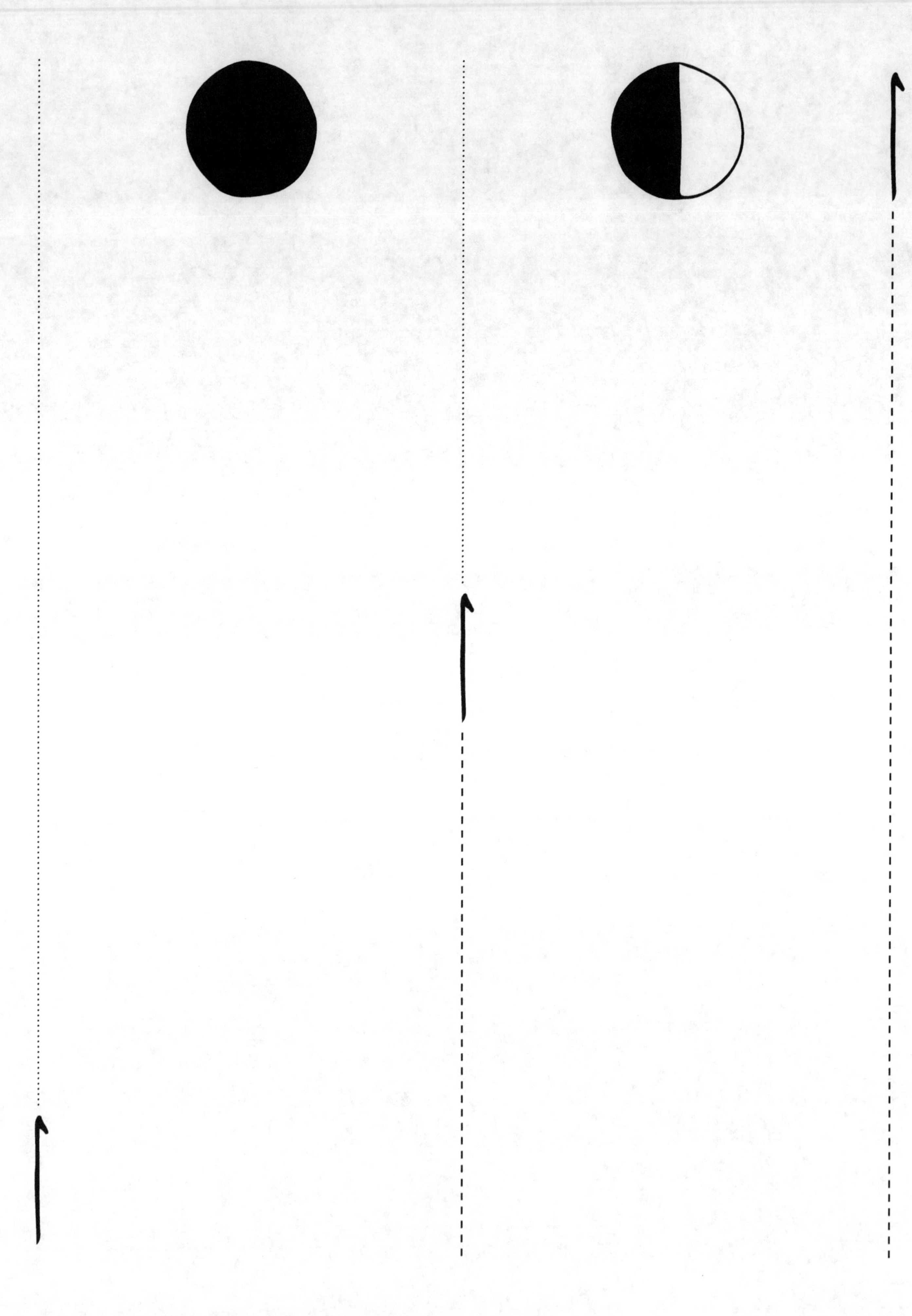

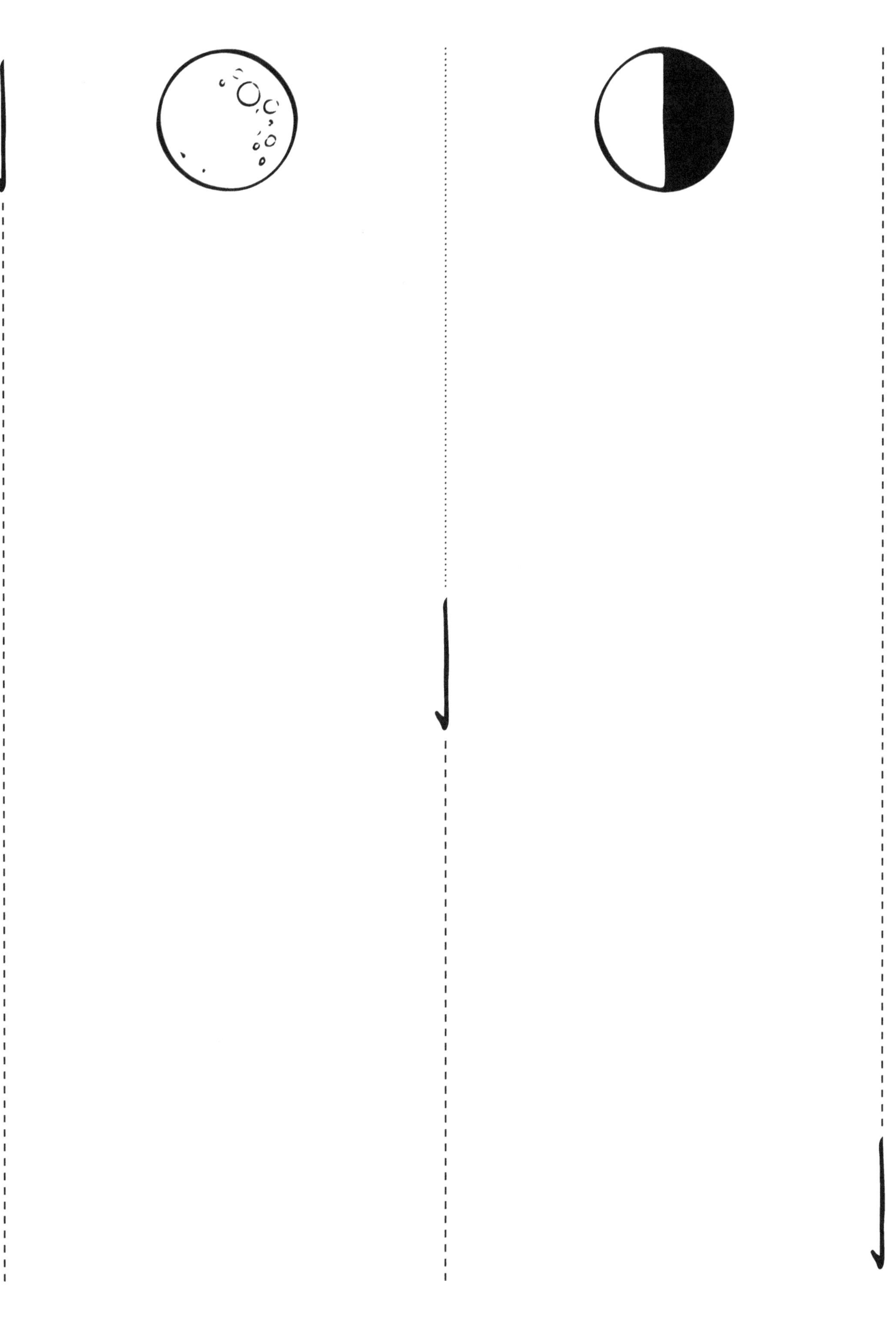

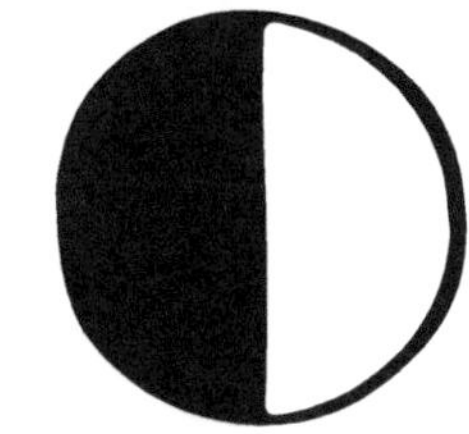

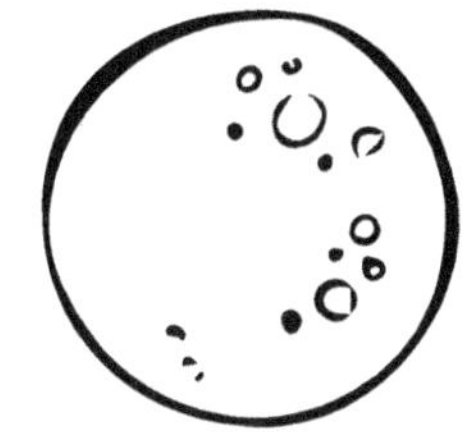

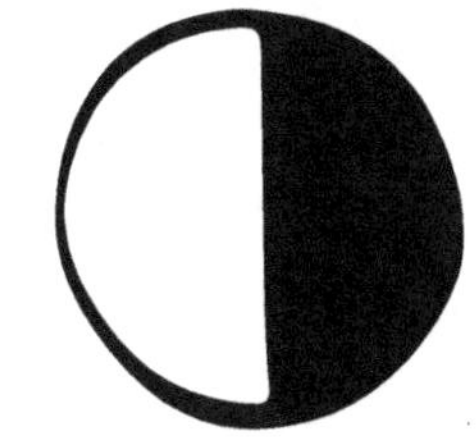

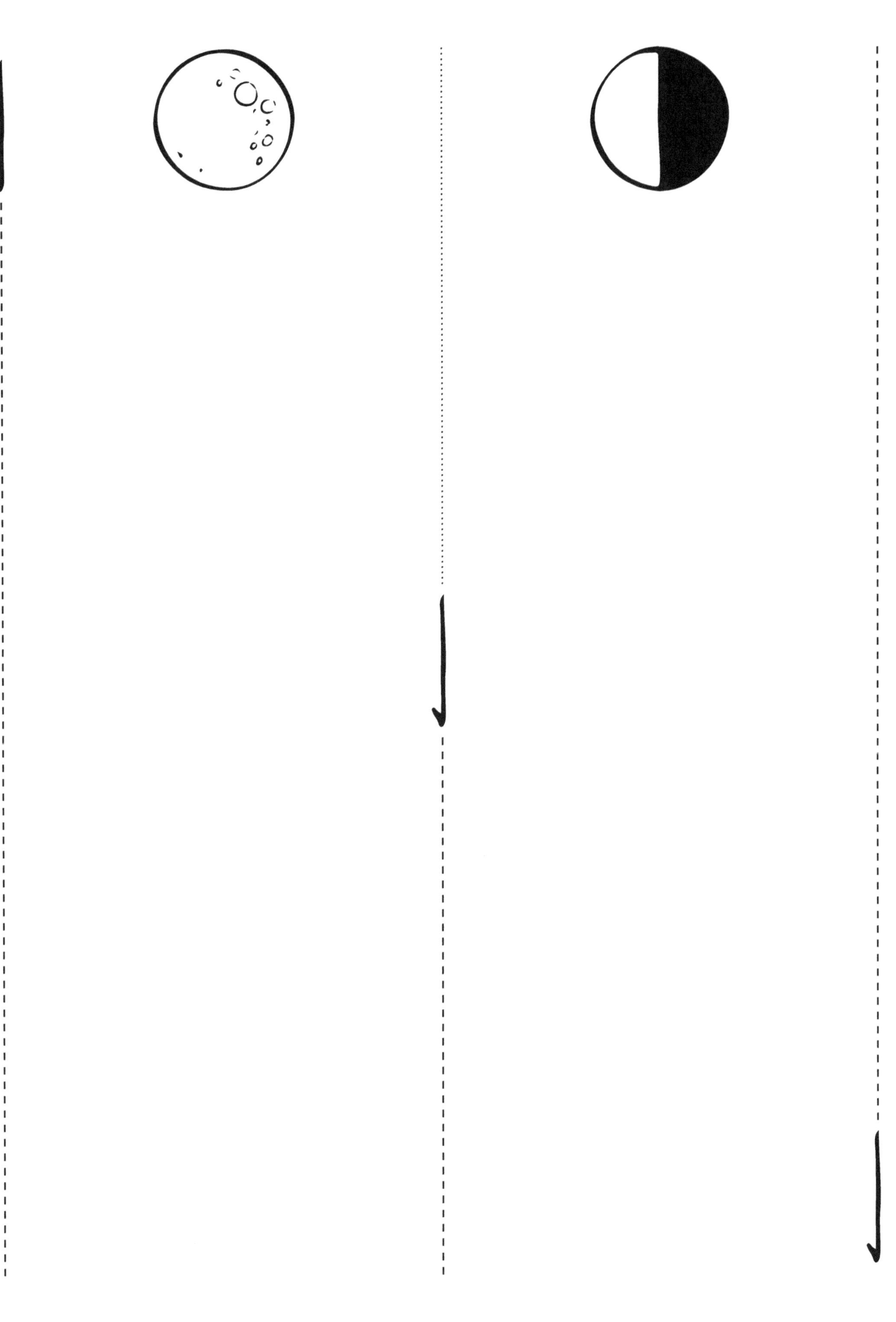

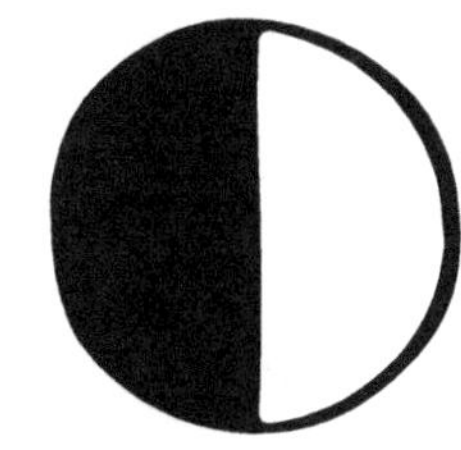

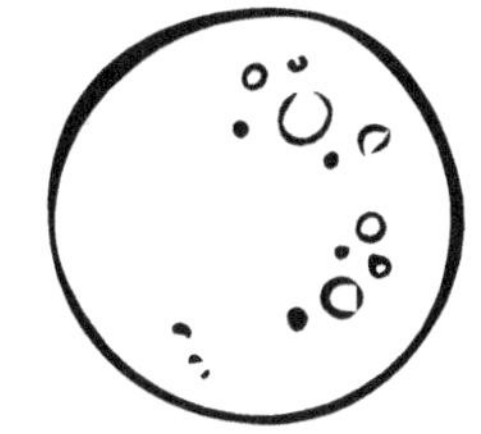

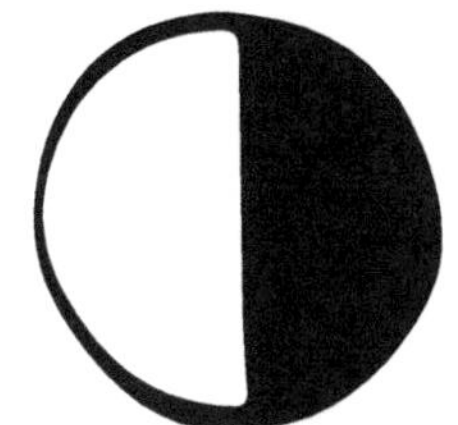

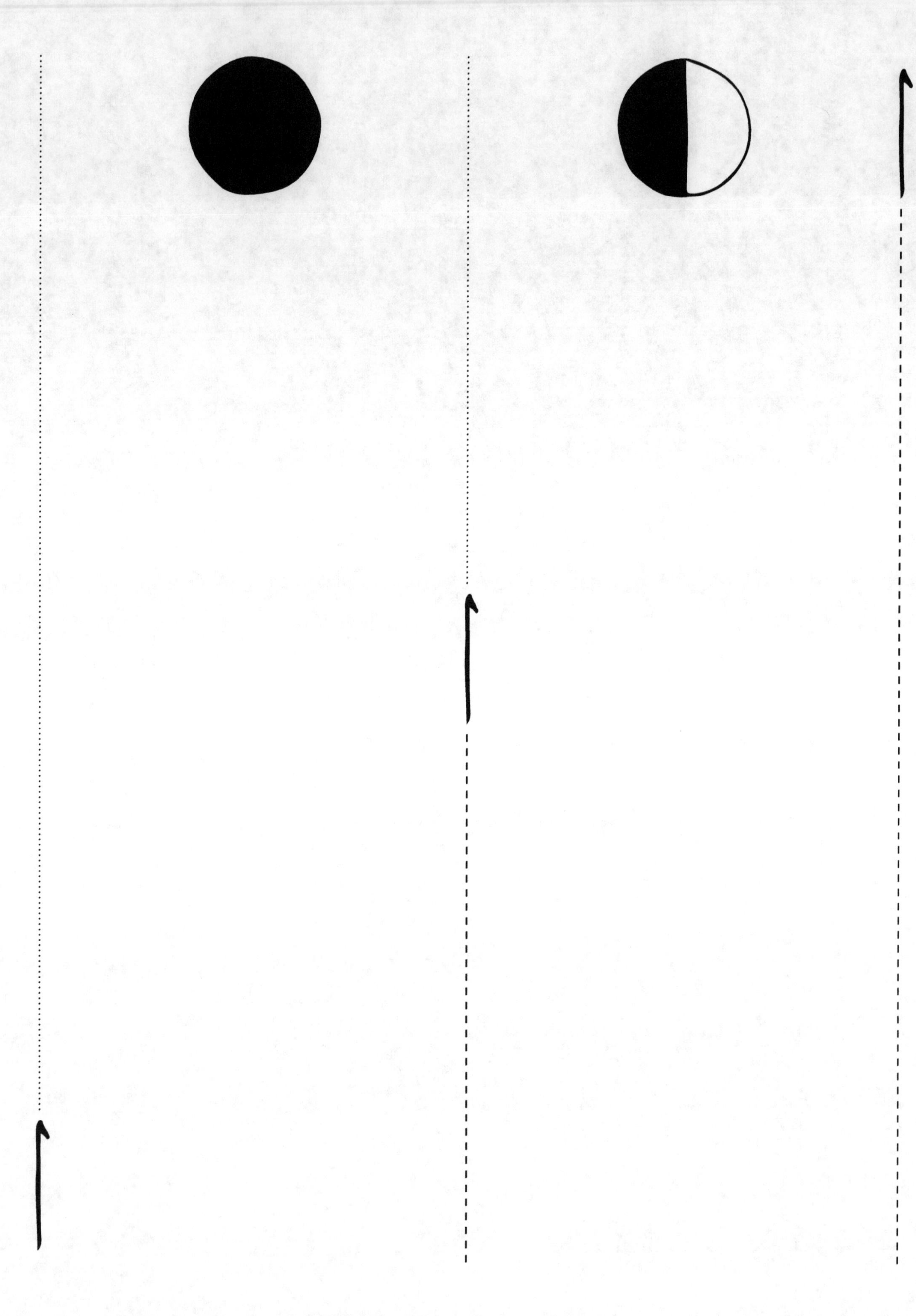

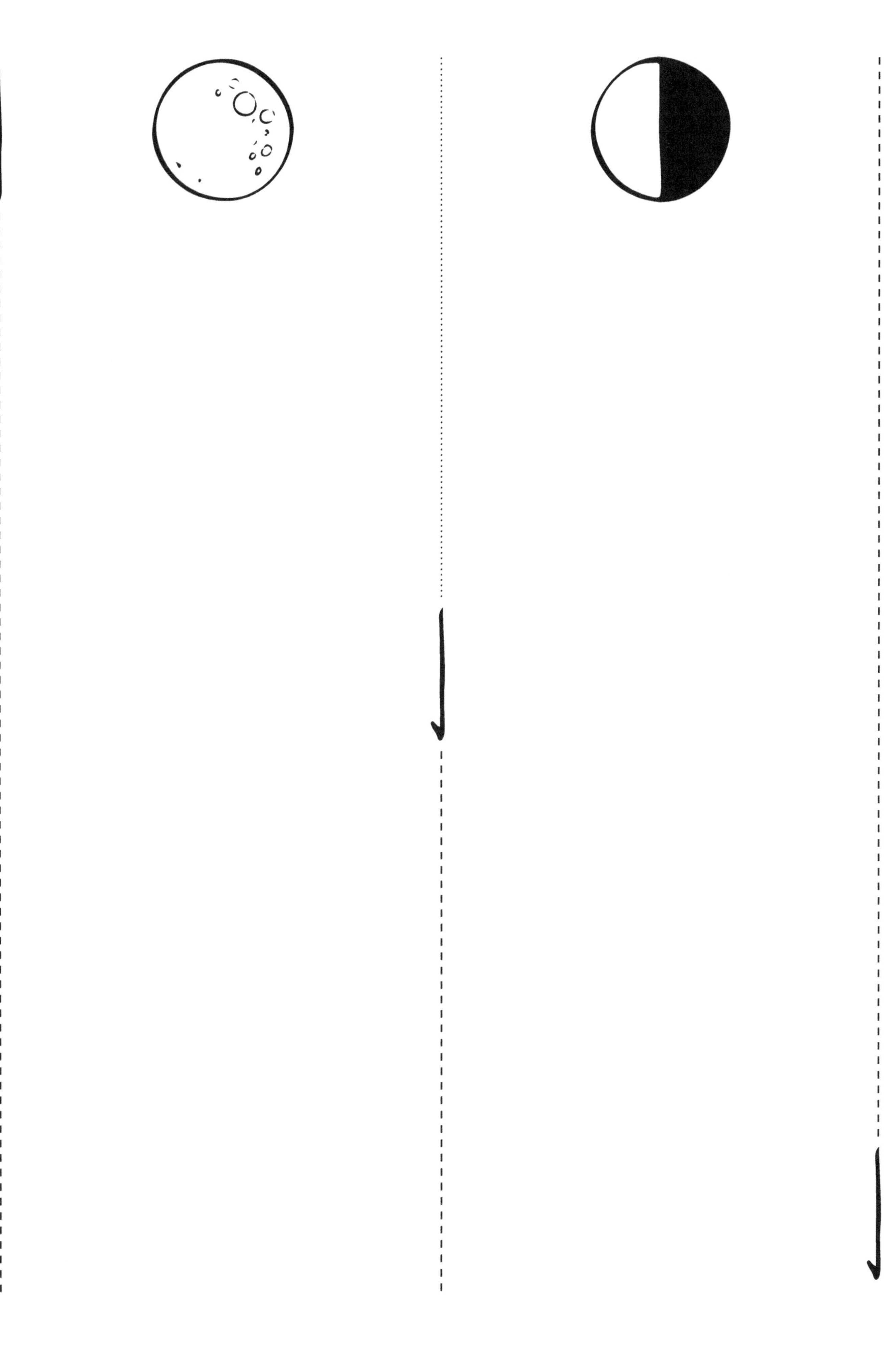

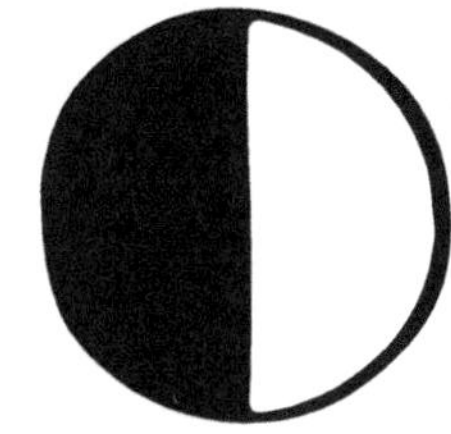

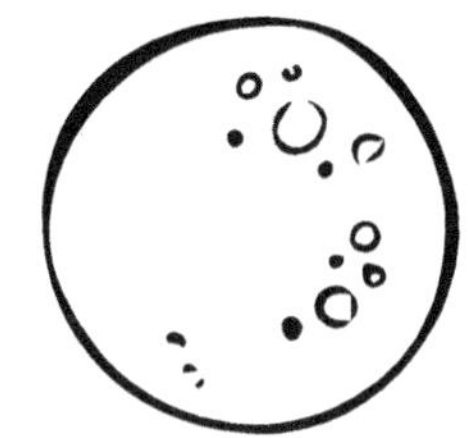

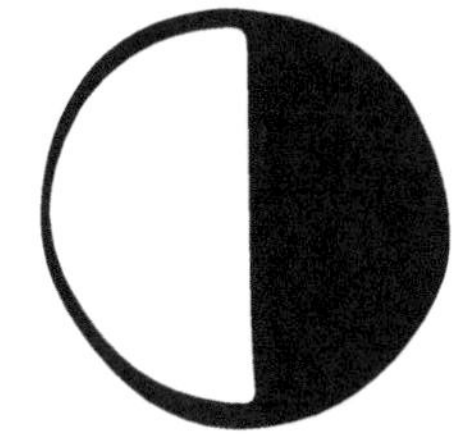

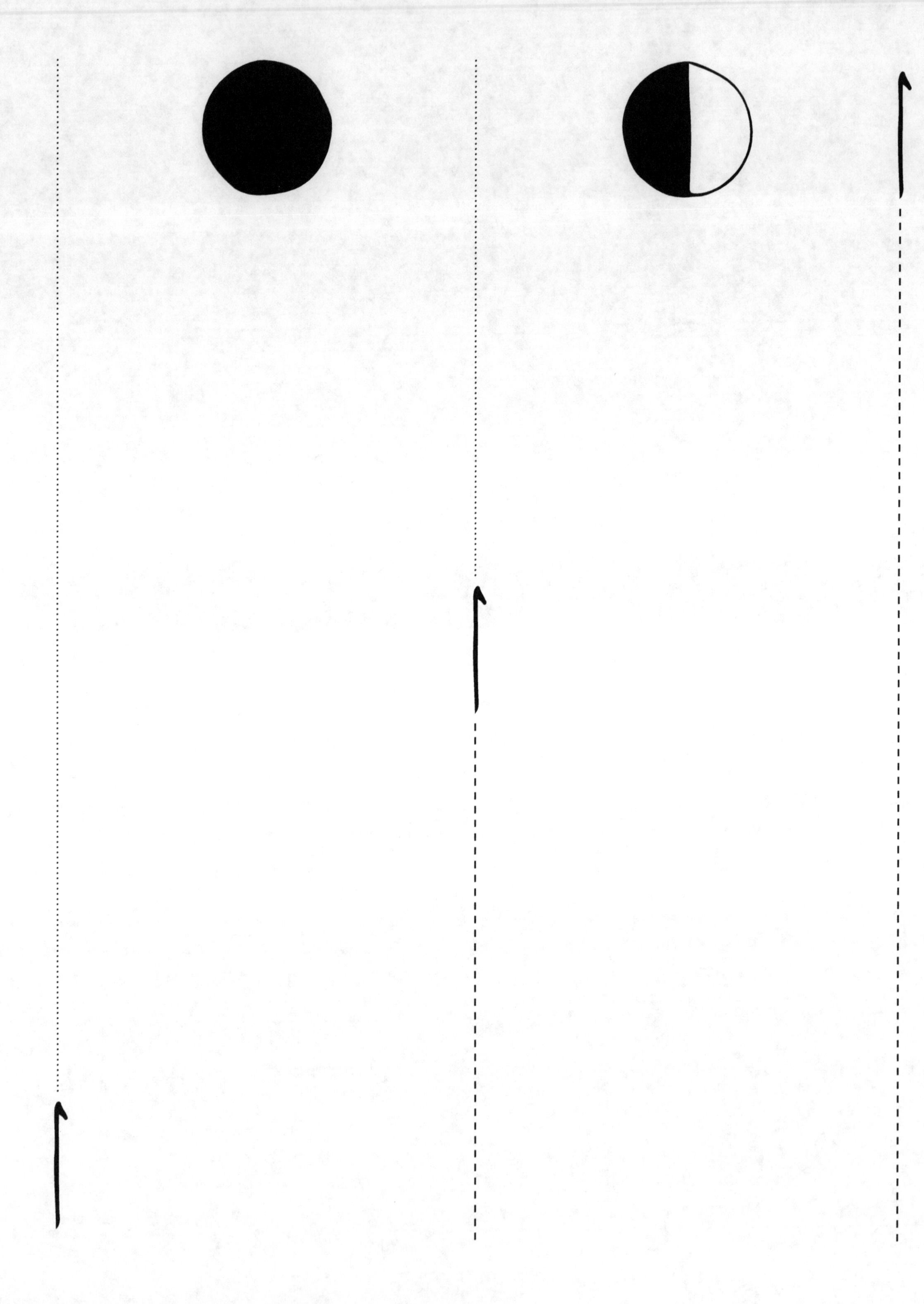

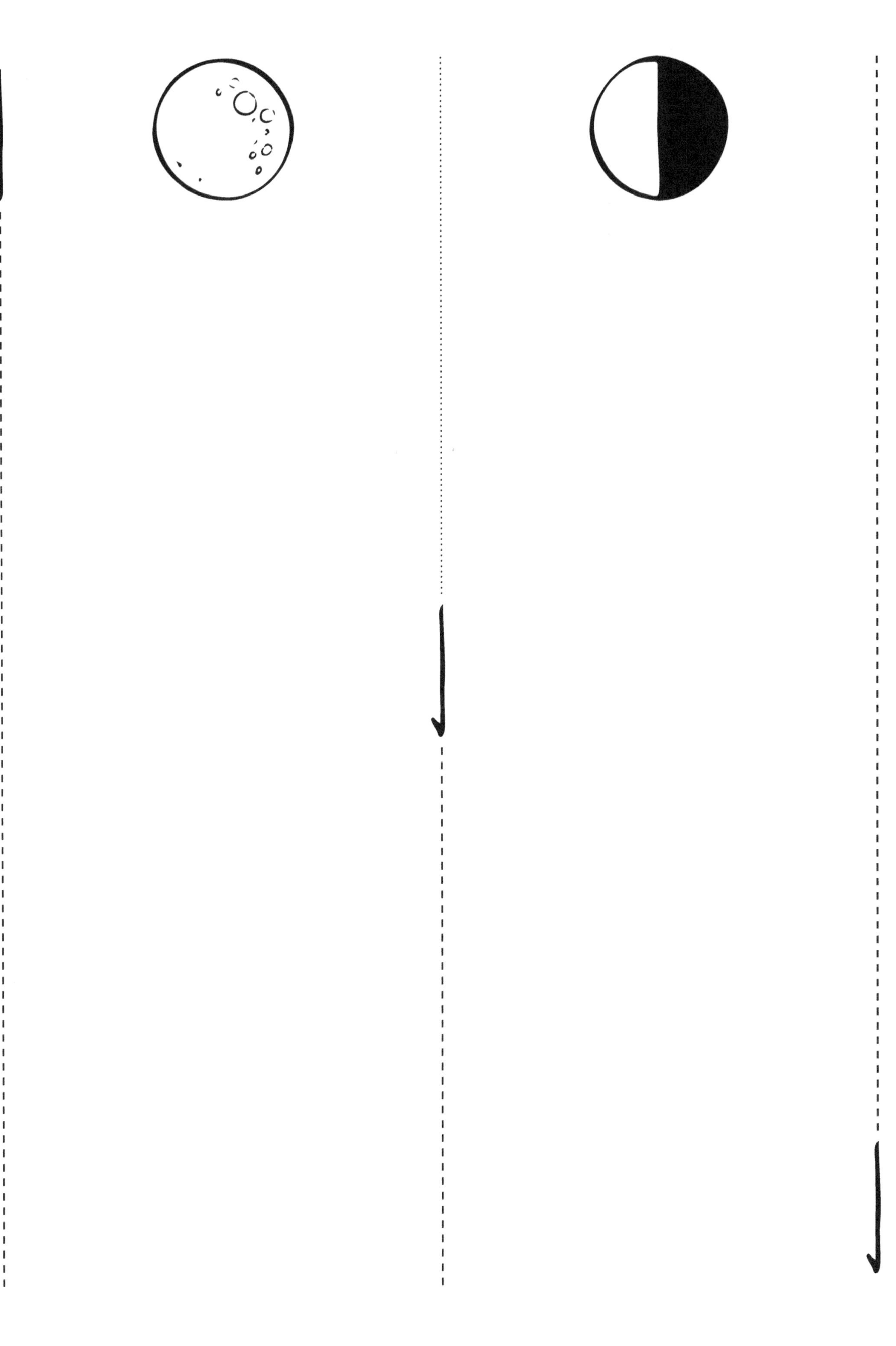

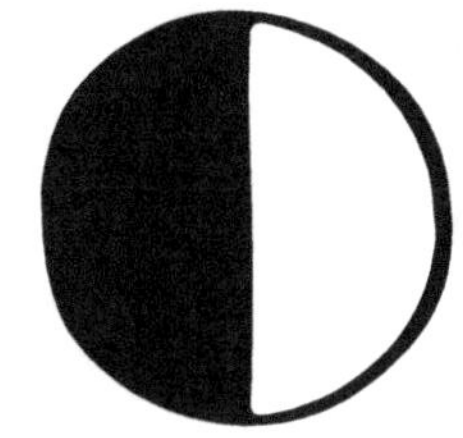

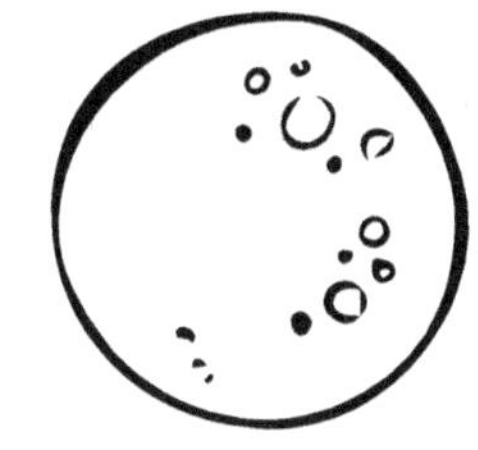

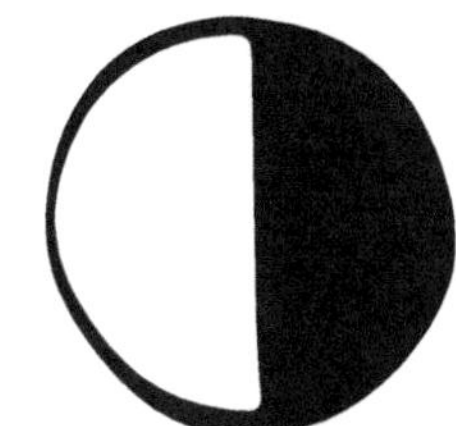

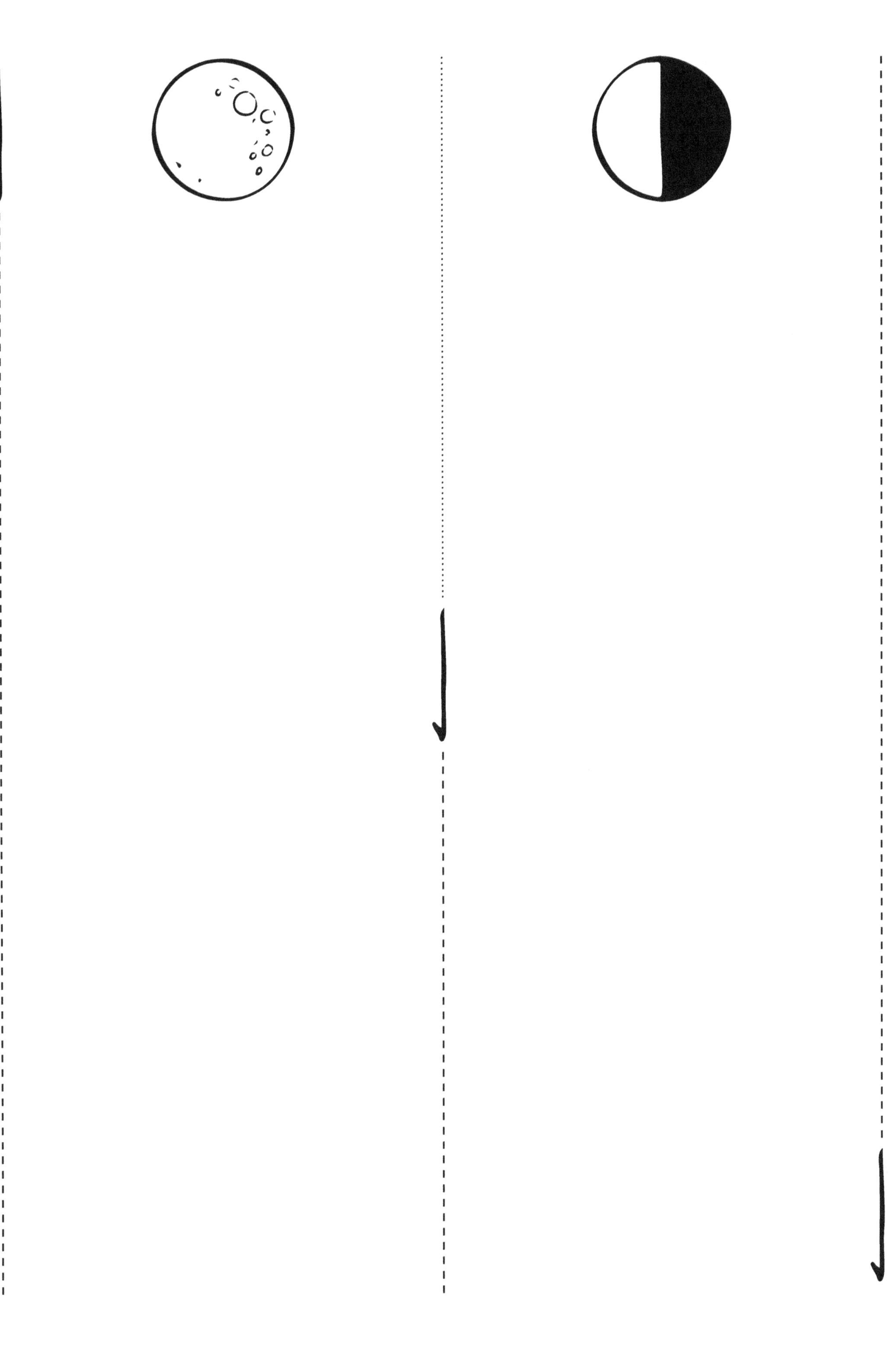

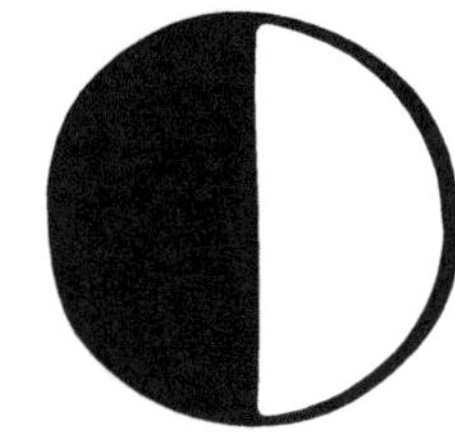

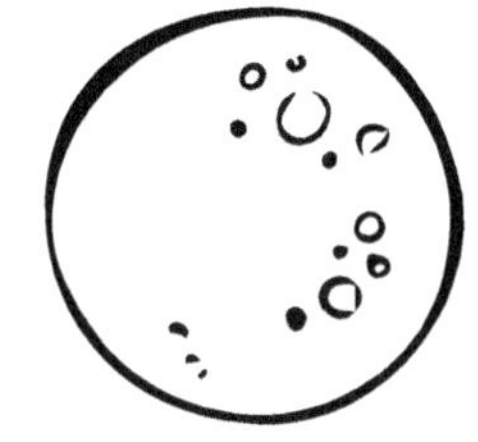

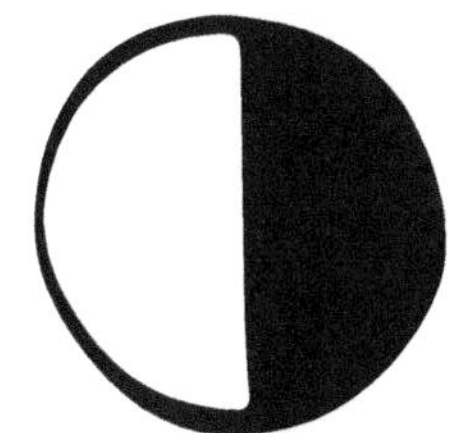

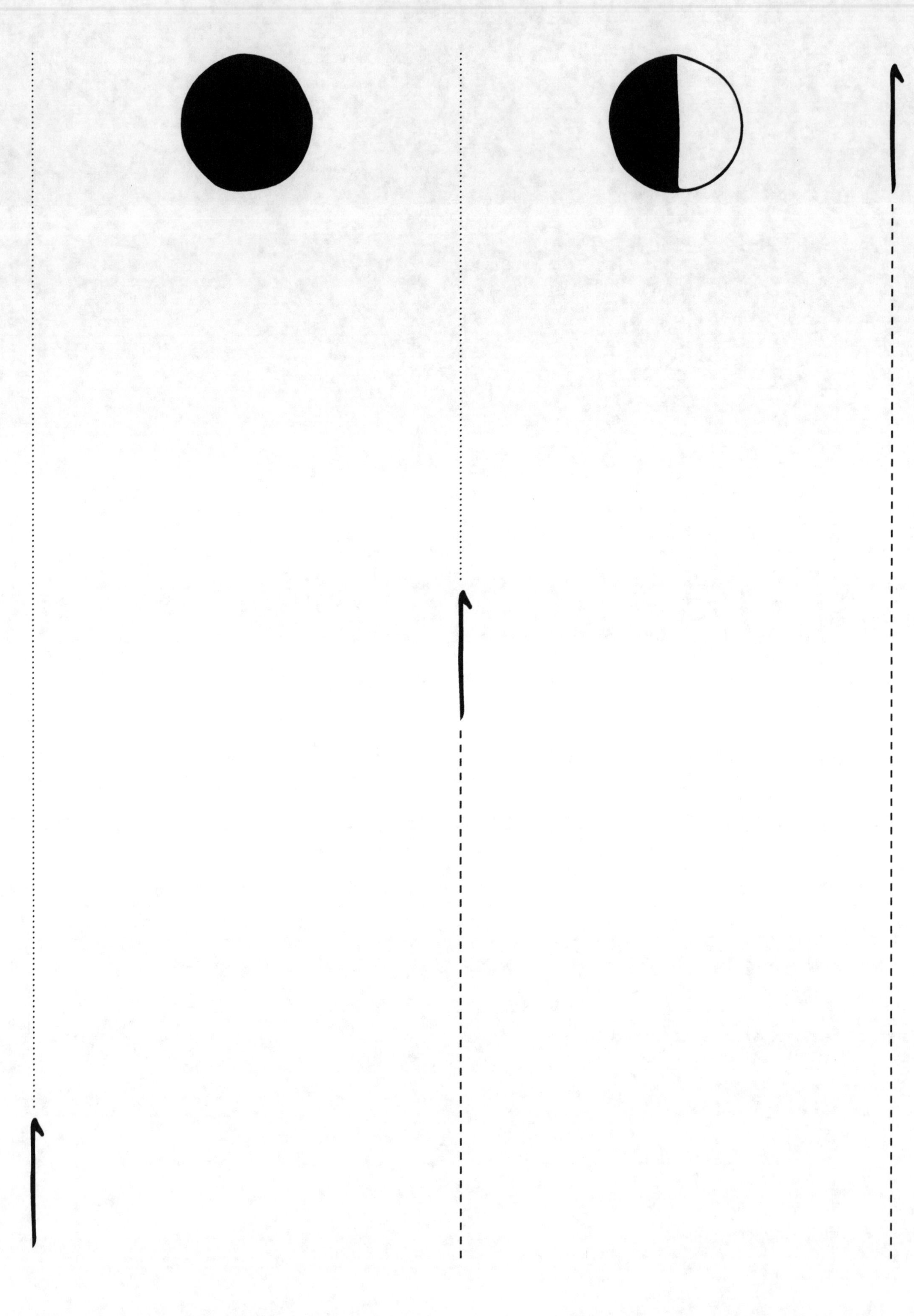

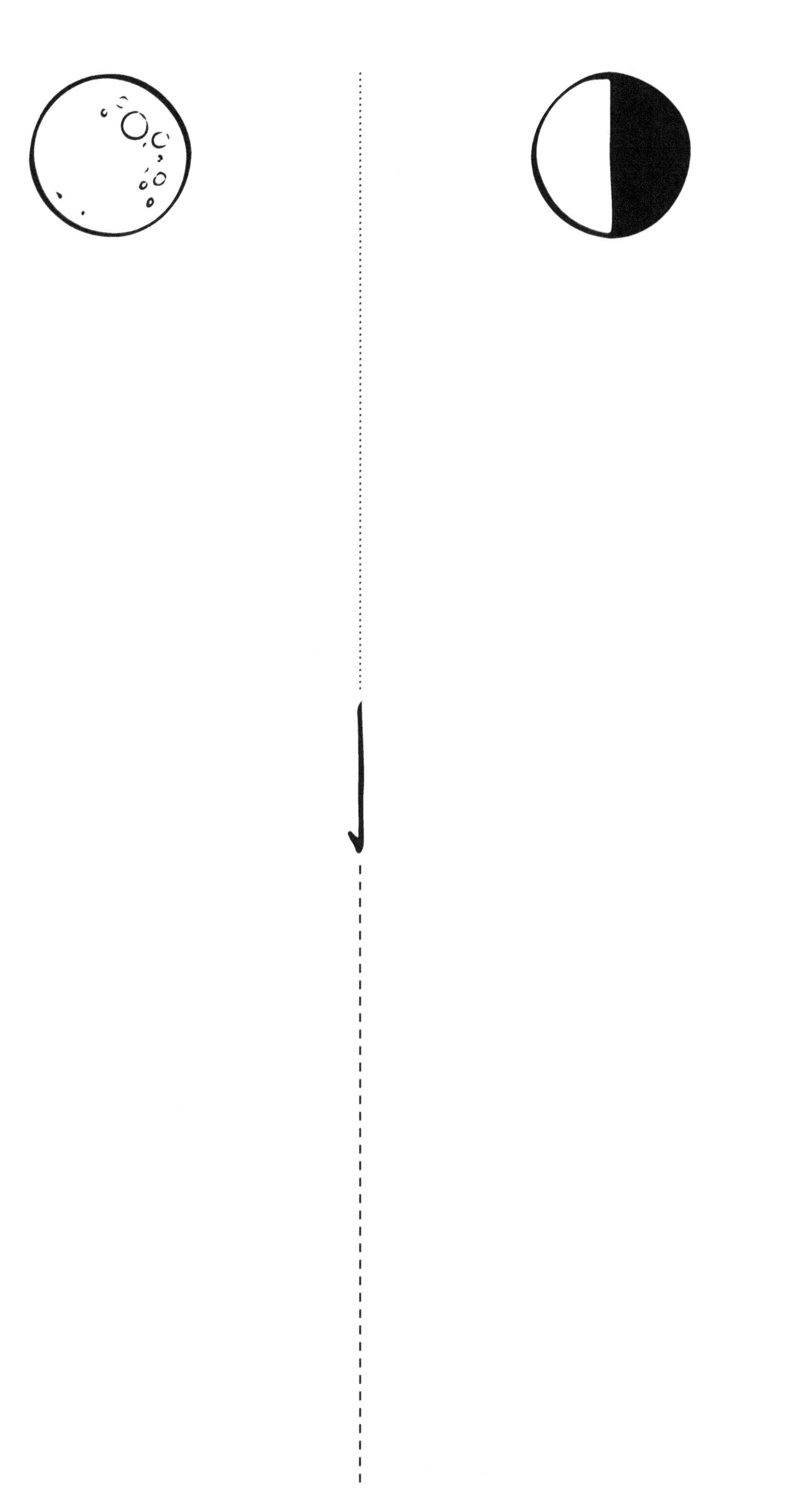

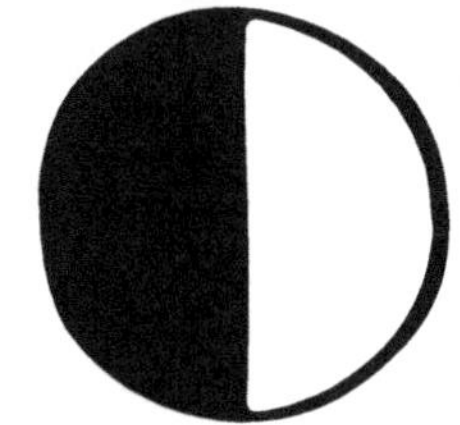

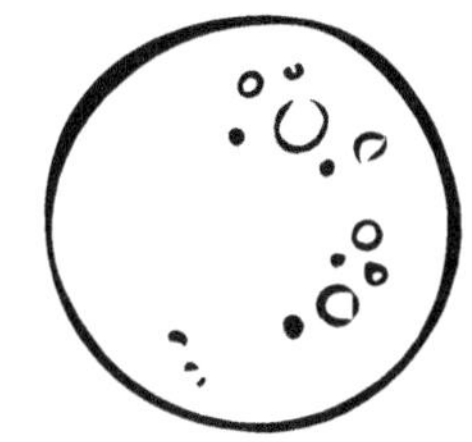

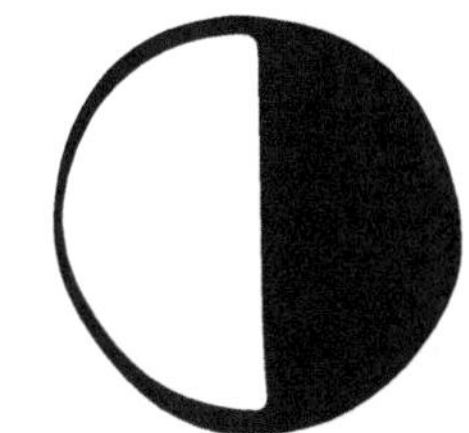

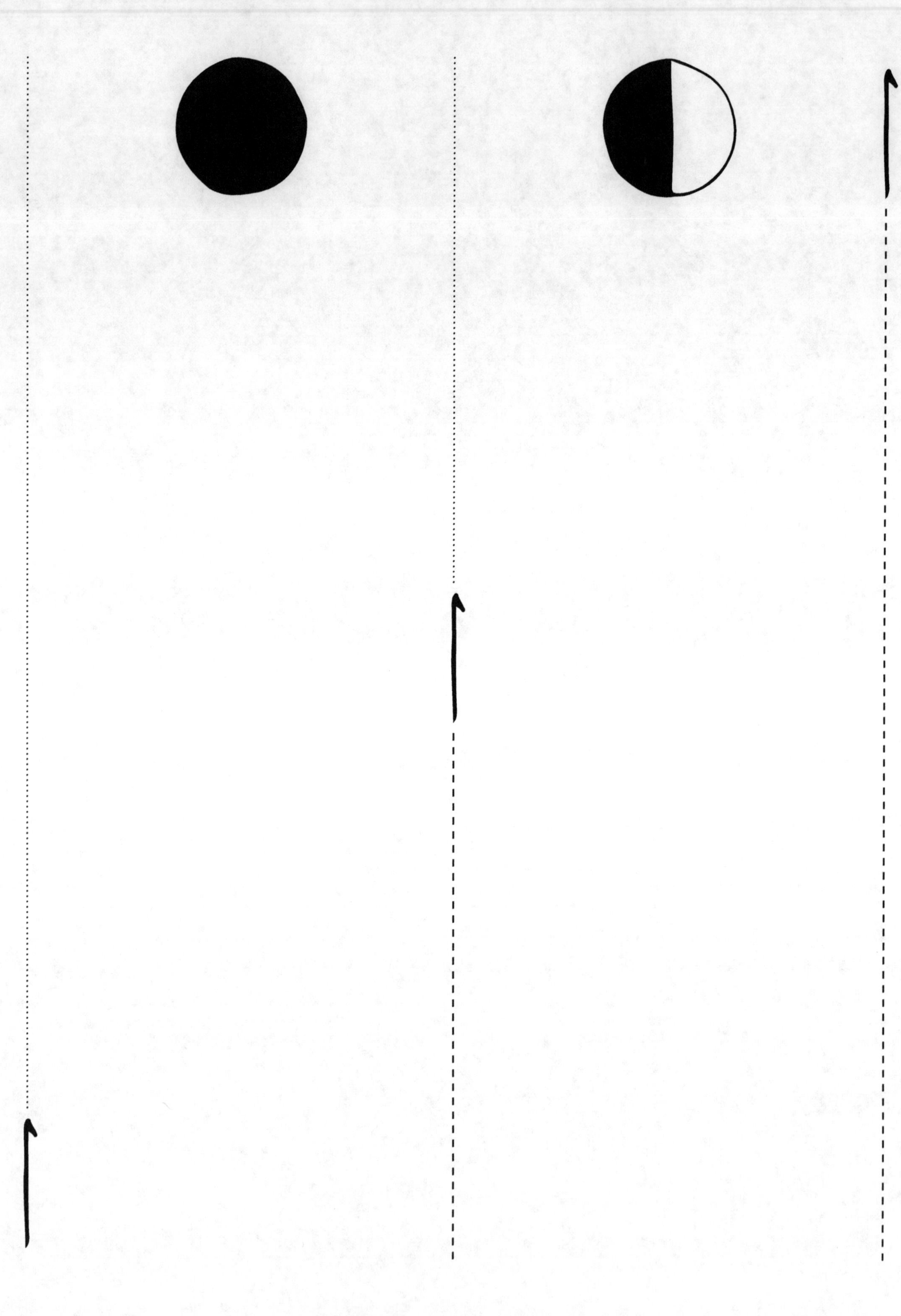

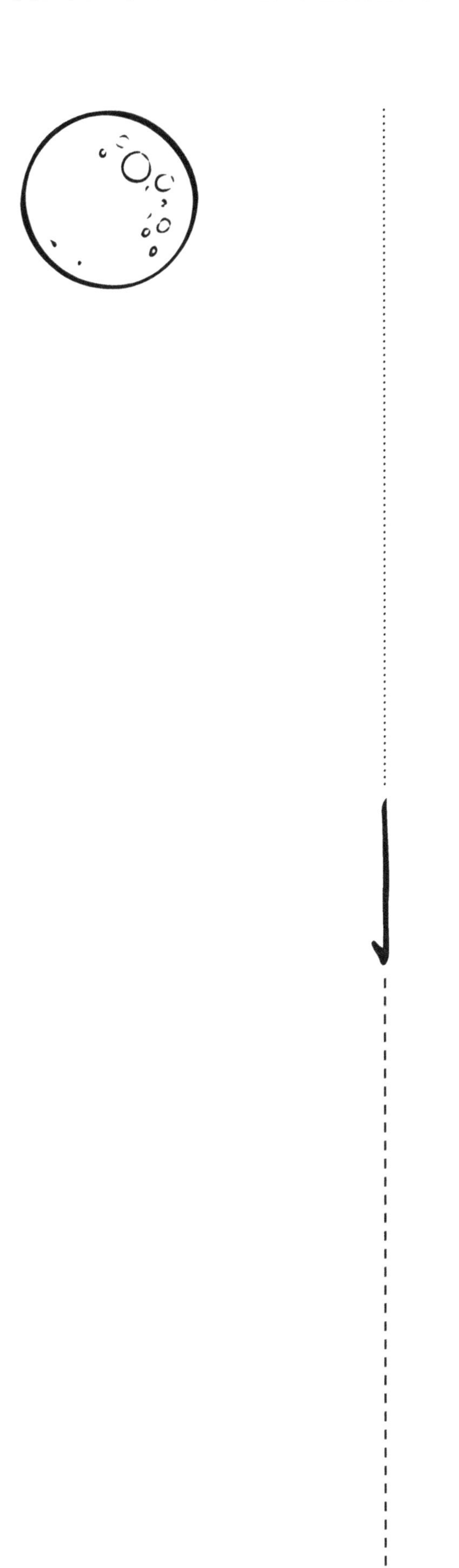
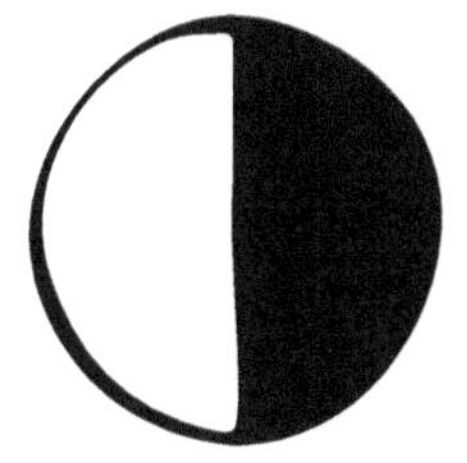

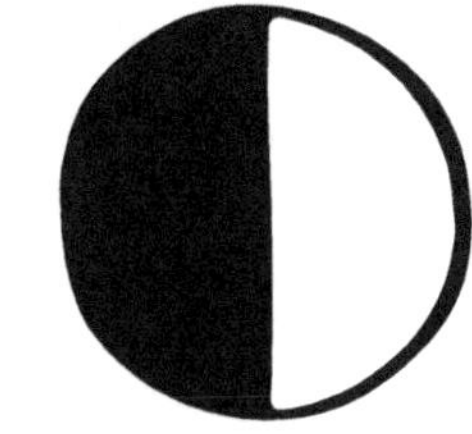

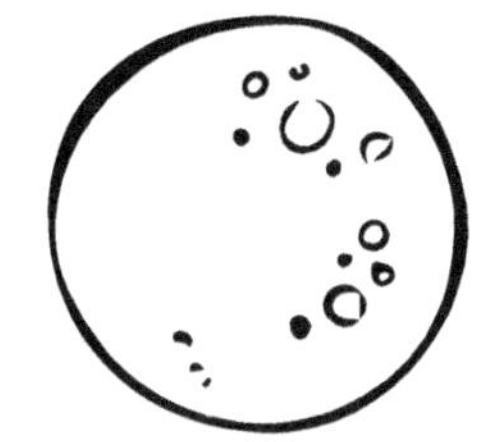

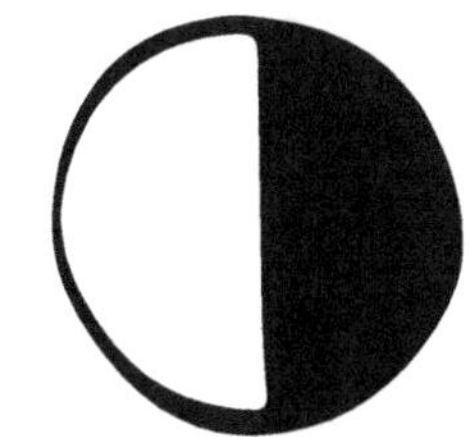